THE MYSTIC MEMOIR:
FROM MIRTH TO INFINITY (AND BEYOND)

by
The Mystic Order of East Alabama Fiction Writers

Village Smith Press
Auburn, Alabama

Copyright 2024
All rights reserved.

No part of this work may be reproduced or transmitted in any form or by any means, whether electronic or mechanical, including photocopying and recording, or by any information storage or retrieval system without the proper written permission of the copyright owner.

1. Anthology   2. Memoir   3. Southern Women

ISBN:
First Edition
9798876613561

Illustrations by Margee Bright Ragland
Layout and design by Cheryl Grisham

Also by the Mystic Order of East Alabama Fiction Writers:

Be the Flame

Not the Moth

The Ploy of Cooking

Mastering the Art of Wench Cooking

Listen to our mystical and whimsical musings on the *Mystic Order Podcast*.

This book is dedicated to all our pirates.

Contents

INTRODUCTION 1

CHAPTER 1
Tender Beginnings
Raised by Wolves • Marian Carcache 5
Jackson, 1953 • Joanne Camp 7
Whispers and Rattles • Mary Dansak 12
What's in a Name? • Margee Bright Ragland 16
Bouncy Houses and Honey Boo Boos • Gail Smith Langley 20
In King Arthur's Service • Katie Lamar Jackson 24
One Tap Over the Line • Gail Smith Langley 27
Rhinestones and Daggers • Marian Carcache 30
Mount Katahdin, 1961 • Joanne Camp 32
Chocolate Monopoly • Gail Smith Langley 37
Mid-Century Man and a Mule Named William • Gail Smith Langley ... 39

CHAPTER 2
Teenage Mutants
It Looks Like I Made It • Katie Lamar Jackson 43
Pepper's Secret • Mary Dansak 45
The Secret Bra • Margee Bright Ragland 49
That February • Mary Dansak 52
Firetruck • Joanne Camp 55
Winged Feet of Mercury • Marian Carcache 59

CHAPTER 3
Enlightenment and Erudition
Cool Kid Rising • Mary Dansak 63
Riding with the Boss • Mary Dansak 68
Spring Break Cruise in Haiku • Margee Bright Ragland 71
Tornado • Joanne Camp 72
Spain, 1974 • Joanne Camp 77
Grad School Confidential • Margee Bright Ragland 82
Whose Shoes? • Joanne Camp 85

CHAPTER 4
Amore or Less

Stalking Mr. Diamond • Gail Smith Langley	91
The Decision • Joanne Camp	94
Ted Nixon, Where Are You? • Katie Lamar Jackson	99

CHAPTER 5
The Royal Issue and Other Children

Fortress • Mary Dansak	105
Low Christmas, High Christmas • Gail Smith Langley	106
A Brief on Child Rearing • Joanne Camp	110
The Year of the Horse • Katie Lamar Jackson	115
Perfectly Composed • Mary Dansak	119
The Hands that Raised You • Katie Lamar Jackson	121

CHAPTER 6
In Your Prime Numbers and Middle Age Crisis

Cruising with the Buckeyes • Gail Smith Langley	127
A Sister's Guide to Grief • Mary Dansak	131
Inspiration Oaks • Gail Smith Langley	134
The Russians Have Come • Joanne Camp	139
Capital Murder • Joanne Camp	143
Umbraphilia and the Loss of Innocence • Katie Lamar Jackson.	154
Road Trip with the Mystics • Margee Bright Ragland	158

CHAPTER 7
Wearing Our Trousers Rolled

The Postman at Sunset • Gail Smith Langley	163
Walking with Nostalgia • Mary Dansak	164
Muffuletta • Joanne Camp	167
Studio 521 • Margee Bright Ragland	171
Missed Notes • Gail Smith Langley	174
Beyond-the-Grave Greens • Mary Dansak	177
A Leaper of Waves Grown Old• Gail Smith Langley	180
Music of the Spheres • Marian Carcache	181
The Age of Potential • Katie Lamar Jackson	183
Preparing to Migrate • Gail Smith Langley	186

MYSTIC BIOS   187

Introduction

Not one of the six Mystics can say how long the group has been together as writers and companions. An uneducated guess would be close to twenty-five years ... long enough for our lives to become entwined and merged, long enough to be sisters without a DNA match. I know these years have made me a more discerning and stronger writer. More importantly, I have gained the gift of five life-long friends.

The Mystic Memoir is our last Mystic book. No, we are not calling it quits, but going back to our beginnings when we brought random works to our sacred first Wednesday meetings in order to delight or give pause to our fellow writers. We will continue to gather each month to read our drying inked pieces, blessings for the listeners.

I think of Robert Frost whose two roads diverged in a yellow wood. For the Mystics, six roads diverged, and I intend to travel all with my Mystic companions.

"I shall be telling this with a sigh
*Somewhere ages and ages hence."**

Gail Langley, Mystic Queen

*Excerpted from "The Road not Taken" by Robert Frost

The Mystic Memoir

Chapter 1
Tender Beginnings

Raised by Wolves
Marian Carcache

I was born during a time of fear, the same year the Air Force was born, but not in time to be delivered in an Air Force hospital. Sixty-plus years later, Mama still claims that "Communist" doctors tried to kill her in Camp Kilmer's Army hospital. "It was infiltrated," she says, still today affected by The Second Red Scare, stirred up by a senator named McCarthy who, like certain politicians still do, made accusations without regard for evidence.

Daddy was stationed in New Jersey, the "Garden State," when I made my entrance into the world. Mama points out that she didn't see a garden the whole time she lived there. Shortly after returning to their small apartment from the maternity ward, Mama got sick, fainted, and almost dropped me. She managed to fall backwards onto a bed and was conscious enough to hold newborn me between her knees so that I didn't hit the floor.

Mrs. Lindner, the German landlady that Mama and Daddy rented their attic apartment from, hearing a thud and terrified baby cries, rushed upstairs to rescue me and call an ambulance to take Mama back to the Army hospital. She had blood poisoning because the doctor had failed to deliver the placenta after delivering me — only adding to Mama's list of evidence that he was a Russian operative trying to kill her. All these years later, I try to tell her that Capitalists, not Communists, are actually the ones who are killing us slowly. She has begun to see that I may be right.

Years before "compassionate leave" was even thought of Daddy had to report to base every morning while Mama was hospitalized. Family had already returned to Alabama after coming to New Jersey for my arrival. That left Mrs. Lindner to care for me, a colicky newborn.

Her solution was to make a crib in a dresser drawer that she placed on the floor. Her faithful German Shepherd, Sabre, lay beside me and kept watch while meticulous Mrs. Linder did her daily household chores.

To this day, I am far more comfortable in the company of dogs than I am with humans. And when my own child was a toddler, he bayed the moon and carried shoes in his teeth as he crawled around the house on his all fours. He even asked me to change his name to Wolf. Imprinting, anyone?

Jackson, 1953
Joanne Camp

"Doctor," Althea whispered, "I can't catch no white baby!"

Althea had just ushered Dr. Bedsole into a corner of the examining room out of the hearing of the young couple. Dr. Bedsole was dressed in a white sharkskin suit, with a pale blue tie and two-toned wingtip shoes. His six-foot body towered over the Black midwife. She wore a blue chambray dress with white stockings. Her hair was pulled back in a white kerchief. A white bib apron was tied around her waist.

"You are going to have to Althea, I don't have time to change," he stated matter-of-factly. Then leaning into Althea, he stated in a low voice, "I don't think these folks will mind."

Dottie, lying on the examination table in the office, let out a deep, groaning yell. "Please," she panted, "this baby is coming."

***

Just two hours before, Dottie had been trying to sleep in their upstairs apartment. Outside in the dark of early morning, a cat yowled to a love interest. The black metal oscillating fan, sitting on a chair at the foot of the bed, pushed the August air back momentarily with every sweep. But the hot, humid blanket returned as soon as the fan swung away. Dottie could feel her one-year-old pressed against her back. His curly blond hair was pasted to his forehead with sweat. On the other side of him, her husband slept in only his shorts, his left arm over his head, and the sheet wadded to one side. The luminescent numbers on the clock on Ed's bedside table showed it was 4:32

a.m. Dottie had been feeling irregular contractions since shortly after going to bed.

She made her way as quietly as she could to the bathroom. The old floorboards creaked at some of her steps, although she barely weighed one hundred and twenty pounds. She hoped she would not wake the landlords.

The young couple lived upstairs from Marvin and Maisie Toland. The Tolands had renovated the second floor of their Victorian home into an apartment. Even though they had lived there for almost a year, Dottie could barely understand their South Alabama drawl. Ed did not seem to have the same problem, and so rather than repeating "pah-don" several times, she just smiled and looked to him for translation. She was sure the Tolands had the same trouble understanding her Rhode Island brogue. Rhode Island, her family, and her friends were over a thousand miles away.

The shower was cool, but the spray warmed quickly as it trickled through her thick dark curls and was almost hot when it hit her shoulders and back. Another contraction grabbed her, and she braced her hands against the wall and ducked her head until it passed. A warm trickle traveled down her legs; it was time. She dressed in a loose summer housedress. Still barefoot, she paused in the hallway as another contraction gripped her.

"Ed," she whispered, as she rubbed her husband's arm, "it's time."

Shortly they were walking down the stairs that ended at the Toland's back door. With a still-sleeping child resting on his shoulder, Ed tapped on the kitchen door window. He pushed his free hand over his crew cut head. He knocked again before Marvin appeared at the door with Maisie shadowing him.

"Sorry to disturb you so early," Ed spoke slowly, "but we have a baby coming." He paused and smiled as the news settled on the still groggy landlords.

"Oh, Marvin, we have a baby coming!" Maisie, who outweighed her thin husband by many pounds, pushed past him and reached for the sleeping child.

"Here." Dottie extended the toddler's diaper bag to Ms. Toland as another contraction gripped her, and she gripped her husband's arm.

"Oh my," Ms. Toland gave a worried look. "Now y'all don't worry a bit about this 'un. You get on to the hospital, straight away. We'll take good care of the little one. Won't we Marvin? Of course we will."

Smiling, Ed nodded and escorted his wife to their automobile parked on the side of the house. Maisie was still calling after them as he closed the door to the 1950 Chevrolet sedan. Away from the chatter, Dottie told her husband, "Doctor said he would meet us at the office."

The closest hospital to Jackson was thirty miles away in Grove Hill. Bedsole had agreed that since Dottie had already had one uncomplicated delivery, he would, as he did with most of his obstetric patients, deliver the baby in his office. The trip was only five blocks from their apartment. Ed parked on the curb in front of the house that was the office and ran around to open the door for his wife.

Light emitted from the two front rooms onto the quiet street. The other houses were dark. Only farmers were up at 5:00 a.m., even in Clark County. As the young couple entered, to their right behind the receptionist's desk sat a black woman Dottie had never seen before in all her prenatal visits.

"I'm Althea. Dr. Bedsole's midwife," the woman said. "Ms. Alice, his nurse, is out of town so he asked me to come." Althea's voice was soft and serene.

"Where's Dr. Bedsole?" Ed asked.

"He's on the way. He lives outside town; it takes him a minute to get here."

Althea assessed Dottie, a thin white woman except for her bulging belly. She had kind green eyes, but Althea could see the worry in them. Directing her to the adjacent examining room, the petite midwife crooned, "Let's get you comfortable, Ms. Dottie. I believe we're gonna have us a baby, real soon."

The smell of rubbing alcohol and antiseptic radiated throughout the room. Althea comforted and reassured Dottie as she fussed around her. Dottie was in a gown and on the examining table by the time Dr. Bedsole arrived.

After he and Althea examined the expectant mother, they had a private conversation.

Ed stood by his wife, holding her hand and occasionally pushing his hair with the other. He turned his sky-blue eyes to Dr. Bedsole, who assured him everything would be alright and, with a hand on Ed's shoulder, stood to the side as Althea attended to Dottie. At the first sight of blood, Ed's knees buckled. The doctor caught him and guided him to a nearby chair.

"Put your head on your knees," Dr. Bedsole ordered. "I'm not picking you up off the floor."

In a few minutes, Dottie's last guttural cry was followed by the bawl of a newborn girl. Althea wrapped the baby in a swaddling blanket and handed her to the doctor for inspection.

"Beautiful, healthy baby girl," the doctor declared. "You feeling better?" he asked Ed, and when the new father nodded, he handed the baby to him.

"What is her name?" the doctor asked. Ed answered admiring his mucus-covered new addition.

Dr. Bedsole walked to his desk across the room and, in his best penmanship, filled in the birth certificate: Mary Joanne Alexander, born 5:30 a.m., August 4, 1953, in Jackson, Alabama.

Whispers and Rattles
Mary Dansak

The crunch of acorns under foot. The click-click of my dogs' toenails on a hardwood floor. The creak of pine trees rubbing against each other in the wind. These are the sounds that drive me wild with calm.

When I was little, I used to curl up with my mama in her floral-sheeted bed and beg her to tell me about the day I was born. I leaned into her and closed my eyes, wrapping myself up in her soft arms that smelled of Jergens Lotion and Joy perfume.

"Well," she would say, stroking my thin dishwater-blonde hair, "it was a beautiful spring day."

With those words, all my insides would begin to tingle, and I would fall helplessly into the zone.

"The doctor pulled down his mask and said, 'It's a girl.' I wanted a little girl; I wanted you. I reached for you, but they whisked you away for your first bath. 'Just a few more minutes,' the nurse said. Then I heard them bringing you back, rolling you down the hall in a little bassinet. The wheels went 'rattle, rattle, rattle,' and each rattle brought you closer to me."

My childhood memories are filled with peculiar and exact thrills: my dad pulling a roll of malted milk pellets from his pocket, the gaiety of the nights my aunt and uncle drove over from Montgomery for games of Cribbage and MasterMind, and this very point in my birth story where my mama lay in a hospital bed listening to the rattle of wheels in the hall.

"Finally, the rattle, rattle, rattle stopped right outside my door, and they brought you in and handed you to me. You were wrapped up like a papoose. My little Moose Caboose."

You would think the part about her holding me for the first time would be what sent me into an oxytocin-induced euphoria. But it wasn't. It was the rattle, rattle, rattle of the wheels on the hospital floor. The wheels must have been uneven to make such a noise. The bassinet must have jiggled and bounced, moving along its crooked mooring. Did the clickety-clacking noise soothe me then?

Even as a tiny child, I clearly was blessed with ASMR, or Autonomic Sensory Meridian Response. For those of us affected — the chosen, lucky ones — specific sounds trigger a pleasant brain-tickling sensation, and we feel soothed, drugged almost, into a state of contentment. The term was coined in 2010, but with or without a name for it, those of us who have it know it. Some people are triggered by sounds like crinkling paper, others by whispers. A scritch of a pencil on a drawing pad might do the trick.

For most of my life I thought I was the only one drawn to these sounds. Then one night, my daughter Anna, about three years old at the time, told me she loved the book, *But No Elephants.*

"Isn't the elephant funny?" I asked. "And the silly lady who has all those pets!"

"I like the sound the pages make when you turn them," she corrected me. And then I knew.

I went straight to my mama, who confirmed her own love of crinkly sounds. I asked our other daughters. They acted like I was the last person on Earth to discover that this was a real phenomenon. They showed me a Christmas gift from their grandmother, my mama. It was a homemade CD titled "Rena's Crinkly Paper Sounds," ninety minutes of rustling tissue paper, tracing paper, and drawing paper, lovingly recorded by my mom.

Now YouTube is full of ASMR videos, which I discovered when I was working in an office and needed to wear headphones to buzz out the conversations around me. Music was distracting, so I googled "library sounds." Maybe, just maybe, someone had recorded them: murmurs and crinkles and whispers. Footsteps. Turning pages. Shelving books. Click, click, click. Sure enough, there it was, a whole selection of recordings made in libraries. People with high-end microphones have captured the whispers and shuffles I love, and so much more. It turns out we are legion. Hear us whisper!

Now my YouTube writing playlist includes library sounds, hands rummaging in purses, fingers shuffling through craft supplies, and my favorite, sixty minutes of someone rearranging bottles of fingernail polish.

Having identified and even named my pleasant addiction, I know what to ask my husband to give me for birthday, Christmas, other gift-giving holidays. All I want is for him to shuffle papers, turn pages in a magazine, or, heaven help me, file index cards in a plastic box while I lie in bed beside him at night, falling asleep in a heaven-sent stupor. I would rather have this than diamonds or gold.

I wonder, hearing the "rattle, rattle, rattle" of the wheels on the squeaky-clean hospital floor, is this what set off my own ASMR, that spring day long ago, just as my mother lay in the hospital bed tingling from her brain to her toes, heart bursting in anticipation of holding her brand new baby girl? Or was it passed on in the genetic code, soothing my tiny self in the sounds of the whooshing, watery swirl of the womb?

What's in a Name?
Margee Bright Ragland

"The rabbit died,"* said my mother. I was eavesdropping on my parents' telephone conversation. I was five years old and so curious about this statement. What rabbit? Why did it die? Why was my mother talking about a dead rabbit?

"What are you talking about, Mama?"

"Just a phrase, Margee, nothing to worry about, however, I do have some exciting news to share with you." (My mother was excellent at quickly changing the subject.) "We are going to have a new baby!"

This was great news as I longed for a baby brother or sister to play with and help take care of. "What will we name this baby, Mama?"

"Well if it's a boy, we will name him after your father, Theodore Russell Benning the Third." Naming a child after the parents was a tradition in my family. I was named after my mother, Loretta Margaret, although they called me Margee. So, the new baby would not be named after my mother.

"What if this baby is a girl?" I asked.

"We will have to think about a name. Why don't you think of a name for your sister."

Wow, what a privilege to name the baby. I knew what we called members of our family was very important to my parents. When I was younger, I called my parents Loretta and Ted because that's what everyone called them. I soon learned that these names were not acceptable, especially to my father.

I remember the day he said, "Margee," or rather "Margaret," the name he called me when he was very serious: "Margaret, you are the only person in the world that can call me Daddy, and you must call me Daddy, not Ted. You should also call your mother Mama instead of Loretta."

I replied, "Okay Ted. I mean, okay Daddy." I loved to joke with Ted.

I needed some time to think about that name for the new baby sister. My favorite place to think, when I wasn't outdoors, was the living room. I loved to jump up and down on the sofa watching myself in the mirror above the sofa. This behavior was frowned on by my parents, but they were poor supervisors. This made sofa jumping easy. I also liked to sing as I jumped. One of my favorite songs was "Oh! Susanna."

Oh! Susanna, don't you cry for me. For I come from Alabama with a banjo on my knee. It rained all night the day I left; The weather was so dry. The sun so hot I froze to death. Susanna don't you cry.

I found those contradictory lyrics so hilarious.

Jump, jump, jump, jump!

My mother's maiden name was Serey. Her family was Irish, and every summer I would visit my hordes of Serey cousins in Kentucky. It was great fun to spend my summers with so many children. Serey would be a great name for my baby sister. Okay, there's one good name, I thought, but I have to have two names.

Wait, "Oh! Susanna" would be a great name too. "Serey Oh! Susanna" or "Oh! Susanna Serey." What a brilliant name!

I ran to tell my mother. "The name for the baby will be Oh! Susanna Serey Benning!"

"That sounds like a fine name," my mother replied, "Let's share this name with your daddy."

My parents discussed my baby name and came back with a compromise. Somehow, they didn't like the "Oh!" part. Babies aren't usually named Oh! They also thought Suzanne was more contemporary than Susanna. Suzanne Serey Benning would be my sister's name.

My sister has always loved her unique name. She thought it was special that I named her. Unfortunately, several years ago, Apple Inc. introduced their helper voice. The voice was named Siri. Apple Siri is not spelled like my sister Serey, but it is pronounced the same. Now my sister's name is uttered by everyone on Earth seeking an answer. I'm not sure if my Serey is still pleased with my choice, but that's what I named her, and I am her proud big sister.

When urine is injected into a rabbit, it makes the rabbit's body react as if it is pregnant. The rabbit's ovaries then develop temporary tissue structures known as corpora lutea and corpora hemorrhagica, which doctors can spot on the ovaries. The phrase "the rabbit died" occasionally pops up as an old-fashioned way of saying a woman is pregnant; however, the urine injection does not kill or torment the rabbit. Unfortunately, the fastest way to check the ovaries is to euthanize the rabbit and dissect it. So, whether the woman is pregnant or not, the rabbit died.

Oh! Susanna
By Stephen Foster

I come from Alabama with a banjo on my knee,
I'm going to Louisiana, my true love for to see
It rained all night the day I left, the weather it was dry
The sun so hot I froze to death; Susanna, don't you cry.

CHORUS
Oh, Susanna, don't you cry for me
cos' I come from Alabama
With my banjo on my knee.

I had a dream the other night when everything was still,
I thought I saw Susanna coming up the hill,
A buck wheat cake was in her mouth, a tear was in her eye,
I said I'm coming from the south, Susanna don't you cry.
I soon will be in New Orleans and then I'll look around
And when I find my Susanna, I'll fall upon the ground
But if I do not find her, this man will surely die
And when I'm dead and buried, Susanna don't you cry.

Bouncy Houses and Honey Boo Boos
Gail Smith Langley

Among the array of puzzling apps appearing on my iPad is Next Door. In a down-sizing frenzy, my family moved adjacent to a Gen X neighbor. Neighbor Gen insisted on adding Next Door to my already bewildering group of online choices. She was well meaning, probably hoping to plunge me into the subdivision's cool groove. My password is her kid's name which, on occasion, I have a difficulty recalling.

I think of this as a very unconventional housewarming gift. What happened to the aluminum foil wrapped, freshly baked pound cake? Yet at times, I am grateful to be at one with the outside world. The app can be interesting with reports of vandalism, theft, stranger danger, unlocked car trashing, and snake identification woes. Occasionally helpful information is offered ... lost animals, councilmen's posts. Best, there's a list of recommended handymen, babysitters, and dog walkers. Still, there are a tiresome number of posts which are uninspiring, leaning toward insipid commentary.

"Hello new friends. My name is Debbie Doolittle. My husband and I have just arrived here from Tyler, Texas." Now this could be interesting if it continued with "where we hurriedly left in the dark of night, escaping a long list of parking ticket fines and other small troubles with the constable."

Sometimes I am totally amazed at the messages. Recently one mother gave an account of a turning-five birthday party for her Honey Boo Boo child. The yard display for the gala included a six-foot balloon arch. You might ask, "How much does it cost to get a balloon arch?" One can expect to pay upwards of $15 per linear foot. Baby Boo Boo's mother is looking at a minimum of $75 for helium decorations. To compliment this pink arch, a company called Yard Lovely Inc. will stake individual letters to comprise an eighteen-foot birthday greeting which includes Honey Boo Boo's name. This addition adds another $100 to the tab, but does include removal, conveniently leaving no recycling for birthday six.

Mom also rented a bouncy house and convinced the university's raptor center to show up with a couple of birds of prey. The cake was a creation by Lofty Bakery, Cakes for the Ages ($200). No mention was made of ice cream in the chronicle of festivities. I'm fairly certain the cold delight was present along with the party favors, and machines producing popcorn and cotton candy. I was overwhelmed simply reading the message and adding up the costs. Lord, what happens when the child turns six?

My fifth birthday party, which admittedly occurred just after the first Continental Drift from Pangea, was a diminutive affair. The celebrants sat at three card tables which had been set-up on the level spots in the backyard. Cake and ice cream completed the menu. Entertainment was provided by the pin-the-tail-on-the-donkey poster. Also, much to our moms' distress, we took turns swinging on the Goodyear tire hanging from a nearby tree. Because every girl child wore her best, and probably only, party dress and the added crinoline slips, there arose a chance of getting dirty and, worse, showing our underpants. I don't know if my panties were a flashy problem during that celebration. I do remember that it was a wonderfully exciting day. Total expenditure for the day? I'm guessing $25 tops.

We must have been docile children to not rail against such lacking. Uncomplicated entertainment was the norm for us. If my brother and I had behaved for an entire day, which was a rare, rare, achievement, our mother would take us to the Dairy Freeze. There, we would be rewarded with a small soft cone of vanilla ice cream in the shape of an upside-down tornado.

To further compensate the uncommon occurrence of angelic children, perhaps a twice-a-year event, mother would drive the woodie station wagon a few miles north of town to the highway that led to Birmingham. A new Holiday Inn, recently completed along with a mesmerizing neon billboard, sat at the crossroads. The brilliantly illuminated sign towered over the building as well as our imaginations. This wonder of the world declared, in neon greatness, the motel to be The Nation's Inn Keeper. Topping this astonishing colossus was a star with radiants shimmering all the colors of the rainbow. Commanding center stage was a large citrine yellow arrow, which streamed from the sign's base toward its top taking a daredevil turn just under the star to point to the unknown. The arrow raced, perpetually moving its golden neon from south to west in a continuous mind-altering display.

Spellbound, I would move my tongue around the ice cream in rhythm with the arrow's pulsations, unsuccessfully keeping the sticky drips from falling to my pinafore. Eventually hypnotized by the Holiday Inn's celestial body, I'd promise myself I would be good again one day soon. This was something my brother could never achieve.

Years later, as my own small child was having a brat fit at Disney World, the top of the entertainment heap for small and large children, the long-gone Holiday Inn sign came to mind. I found myself longing for the simple days before apps, bouncy houses, and Honey Boo Boos.

In King Arthur's Service
Katie Lamar Jackson

I was three at the time, so I remember only snatches of living in the gloomy house set deep in the dark woods. But I vividly remember the blood and it was mine.

The house itself was large and imposing, imbued with a fairy-tale mystique, at least in my child's mind. But it had never harbored knights or maidens or magicians. It had simply been the home of a university professor and his wife, a childless couple who had populated their lives with adopted four-legged children ranging from track-weary greyhounds to tatter-eared cats to cast-off nags.

When we moved in, the house had been long-empty, and the forty acres around it even longer neglected following the untimely death of the husband followed some years later by the passing of his deeply bereft wife. Before she died, the wife had willed the house and property to a small church-run college, a generous bequest with only one stipulation: the college could not take possession of the property until the last animal heir died.

By the time of our residency there, all the dogs were chasing rabbits across the rainbow bridge, though their leashes remained, hanging in a neat row on the moldy, murky garage wall and looking to me as if they were waiting to take ghost dogs for a walk. At times I could even imagine their vaporous canine-shaped spirits gamboling at the door, long tongues lolling exuberantly from narrow muzzles as they waited for someone to take them on an outing.

There was, however, still one living heir, a horse named King Arthur, who was in sad shape. My parents had negotiated with a local real estate agent to reduce their rent in exchange for cleaning up the overgrown property and tending to King Arthur's most basic needs, food and water. Instead, my mother, an animal lover with a special fondness for horses, set about doing much more for the steed. After he was wormed, his teeth floated, and his hooves trimmed, King Arthur was soon feeling much better, thank you, much to the dismay of the preacher and the realtor, both of whom desired him a speedy demise.

Young as I was, I already shared my mother's love of horses and often accompanied her to the barn where I could admire King Arthur. I have no photos of King Arthur so I can't be sure, but in my memory he was a giant — well over fifteen hands — and the same red clay color of his paddock. His long mane and forelock and the riot of overgrown whiskers on his muzzle made him look wild and wise all at once. I thought he was beautiful because ALL horses were beautiful to me. (They still are.)

It was during one of these forays to the barn that Mom placed me in the wooden feed trough of King Arthur's stall, safely out of the way of his shambling hooves, while she retrieved his flake of hay. As she stepped out of the stall, he moseyed in and came straight to my perch. When he bent his bristly muzzle toward me, I thought he meant to say "hello." He apparently thought my yellow-blonde hair was hay and, instead of nuzzling me with those wild, wiry whiskers, he bit down on my forehead.

I recall blood flowing into my eyes — my blood — and I remember screaming. Mom came running in, scooped me up, and ran hell-bent-for-leather to the house, her hand pressed against my profusely bleeding wound with a forcefulness born of maternal panic.

Once she staunched the bleeding and knew the wound was superficial, however, my mother's adrenaline-soaked concern turned into amusement. She began to laugh; I like to think it was a laugh of relief.

"I wonder how you tasted?" she said.

Mom, always an advocate for animals over people, then set about defending King Arthur. "He is almost blind, you know. It was just a mistake. I'm sure he didn't mean to hurt you."

Apparently, Mom's explanation placated me because, by that afternoon, I was back at the paddock offering my flattened palm to King Arthur and relishing the tickle of those epic whiskers on my skin as he frisked me for hidden treats. Any fear of him I might have harbored was gone.

The wound, however, never vanished. I still have the scar to this day, more than six decades later, right at my hairline, and I cherish it more than any other mark on my body, of which there are plenty, most of them the results of other encounters with horses.

To me, all those scars are memory maps of my equine adventures, but King Arthur's mark will always be my favorite, proof that, once upon a time, my blood was spilled for the mythical King Arthur.

One Tap Over the Line
Gail Smith Langley

I once tap danced to "Jesus Loves Me." I was six and in the first grade. I had a solid half-a-year of lessons under my belt and one recital that I personally thought went exceptionally well. Before curtains up, Mother had coached me into smiling while performing our class's one routine. I might have overcompensated with a Phyllis Diller grin pasted to my face for the entirety of my excellent tapping gig. The audience seemed pleased.

Not long after my debut, Aunt Kathleen, the acknowledged beauty of the family, was visiting. I so wanted to impress my beautiful relative. By the time Mother and Kathleen had settled on the veranda, sipping their minted iced tea, I was dressed and ready to perform in my dance attire which was fashioned with layers of netting sewn to a beige bathing suit. My tap shoes were sprayed silver. Topping off the outfit was a hat styled with the same netting fanning across my young head. In retrospect, I think my multi-netted costume made me look like an extra chubby, flamboyant, bottle brush. I was ready for my unsolicited performance.

While my mother and aunt endeavored to enjoy their summer beverage, and a long overdue visit, I danced my little heart out on the small concrete platform that was our 1950s patio. For added effect I attempted to breathlessly sing most of the lyrics from the 78 record we had practiced to in dance class. I shuffled and hopped to the snappy tune, "The Darktown Strutters' Ball":

I'll be down to get you in a taxi, honey
Better be ready about a half past eight
Now, baby, don't be late
I wanna be there when the band starts playin'
Remember when we get there, honey
I'm gonna dance off both my shoes
When they play "The Jelly Roll Blues"
Tomorrow night at the Downtown Strutter's Ball.
(Shelton Brooks, 1917)

    As the last tap trailed off, the ladies daintily clapped. The aunt was at least tolerant of my pursuit of her approval. Sadly, I had demonstrated my entire repertoire. Still, encouraged by their endorsement, I decided to continue with a spur-of-the-moment encore. Other than "The Darktown Strutters' Ball," I knew few songs by heart. "Jesus Loves Me" immediately sprang to my young mind. Looking back, it was not one of my better ideas, and not one I'm proud of, but after all, I was six and desperate for the approval of the lovely Kathleen.

    I will add here that my beginners' class was not far beyond a routine consisting of shuffle, ball change, repeat, repeat. Step-heel, step-heel, repeat, repeat. With this elementary skill set, I began to sing "Jesus Loves Me" while monotonously dancing the few steps I knew until, desperately short of breath, I took my bow. My audience of two appeared unhappy. Mother was flustered, and Kathleen must have found her tea to be bitter.

    I am amused at the memory of this childish miscalculated production. Even with mother's scolding and my aunt's disapproval, I insisted I'd learn the choreography to "Jesus Loves Me" in my ecumenical tap dance class. In hindsight, I know that, although Jesus loved me, perhaps Aunt Kathleen did not.

Rhinestones and Daggers

Marian Carcache

Long before wild-eyed Judge Jeannine and pony-riding Roy Moore made spectacles of the robe, I realized that judges are not necessarily just, wise, or even qualified. My first encounter with judges, mind you, had nothing to do with the judicial system. They were the community leaders who presided over the Little Miss Bluff City pageant that all second-grade girls participated in.

It seemed a travesty to my seven-year-old mind that Linda MacEwen won the contest because she was not prettier, more congenial, or more talented than the rest of us. She wasn't even from here; she was a "move-in," a "passer-through," whose daddy had a job at the radar base. I was baffled. Maybe she prayed to win, I reasoned.

Her "crowning" (forgive the pun) peccadillo in my child mind was that she wore her mousy hair rolled in pink sponge rollers to school the day of the contest. Along with smoking on the street, having fake fingernails, accessorizing with rhinestones during the daylight hours, picking one's nose or scabs, and licking an ice cream cone in public, wearing curlers to school was a sure indicator of bad taste in Alabama in 1961. Girls weren't allowed to wear long pants to school even in the coldest of winter, but Linda was given a pass on wearing curlers to school at Bluff City Elementary — and then rewarded with the coveted title that evening.

I wondered if the local citizens named as "impartial judges" — a coach, a businessman, and a music teacher — knew that she cleaned her fingernails with her teeth, and probably vice-versa.

My grandmothers, Mamama and Mama Brown, had bought yards and yards of pink satin and net and several spools of pink velvet ribbon. They tediously fashioned rosebuds to garnish the dress I would wear to compete for the title of Little Miss Bluff City. I know they must have been disappointed in the pageant's outcome, too. Of course, I knew if I said a word about Linda winning, I'd be reprimanded for "sour grapes."

Truthfully, I didn't really blame Linda. I only wanted that tiara because it sparkled so pretty when the overhead lights in the auditorium frolicked around on its rhinestones. Linda was as innocent of wrongdoing as I was, both of us little girls growing up in a world that taught us to compete against each other for things that sparkle. The adults involved were the ones who lacked judgment.

The travesties I have seen "Justices" sanction over the years have been far more devastating than a second grader with an eye for rhinestone tiaras could even imagine. Long ago, I traded in my longing for a shiny crown for a razor-sharp box cutter safely tucked in my boot.

Mount Katahdin, 1961

Joanne Camp

"Who is that?" I asked, pointing to a wanderer hiking on the side of the road.

My father smiled. "The Old Man of the Mountain."

As our 1960 Chevrolet station wagon slowly passed the hiker, my brother David leaned over me and out the window and shouted, "Hello, Old Man of the Mountain!"

"David! Get back in the car," my mother chided.

The man walked at a steady pace, a staff as long as he was tall in his hand. He was dressed in a long black coat and had a large leather-brown backpack. His hair was long and grey fading to white and topped with a wide-rimmed black fedora. His beard was the same color as his hair and lay on his chest like a bib. He ignored my brother's greeting as we drove by.

Cool air blew into the car. I rested my head on the door, and the breeze tangled my blonde hair. My four brothers and I shared the back seat, with two weeks of groceries and all the camping gear we would need for our vacation in the Maine woods behind us. Being the oldest, I claimed one of the car's windows. My oldest brother, Jimmy, had the other. Between Jimmy and David, the next in age, Peter dozed. He had been asleep for most of the trip. Mark, the youngest, was wedged in between. We were all stair-step children, just five years between me and two-year-old Mark.

My parents had loaded us in the already packed car early that morning. Excited about the trip, we ate the Sugar Pops breakfast only after constant cajoling. The hum of the long stretch of driving Interstate 95 from Rhode Island to Maine soon had us dozing or sleeping again, but the bump and jostle of leaving paved highway brought us all awake.

The scenery changed from asphalt and blasted rock to gravel and trees, with the occasional lone boulder sitting in the middle of a grassy field. As our drive climbed, the road narrowed and twisted. We rolled the car windows down and absorbed the landscape as we began following along a river, wider than the road we were on.

Dad stopped at a log and stone building, disappeared inside, and soon emerged with a man dressed in brown with a hat like Smokey Bear. He smiled and waved at us all as we pulled away and continued up the winding dirt trail where we had seen the old hiker.

Farther down, my father pulled into a clearing in the forest. We tumbled out of the car to view our surroundings. Trees, pines, and oaks defined our campsite on three sides. The smell of pine and earth perfumed the area. Across the trail was a field of tall grass and wildflowers, and beyond that the river. We ran and leaped like lambs in Spring. I gathered yellow, red, white, and blue flowers until my hands could hold no more. My father's voice reined us in: "Let's get this car unloaded."

We unpacked what little we could as my parents carried a large box and dropped it with a thump. From it, they began unfolding a heavy green canvas tent. My parents struggled with the weight while fixing the center pole. Giving each able child a rope attached to a corner, we erected our home for the next two weeks. To our childish eyes, the tent was as big as our house. A double sleeping bag was laid out on each side of the center pole — one for us and one for our parents.

That night, over the campfire, my mother made a pot of what we called American Chop Suey — macaroni, ground beef, and tomatoes — with her special spices. We ate like the wildlings we were becoming but could not empty the cooking pot. Then lulled by the campfire and hot chocolate and dressed in sweatpants and hoodies, we crawled into the sleeping bag at dark. The Maine nights were cold, but with the sleeping bag and body heat, we slept like squirrels in a nest.

The next morning as we crawled out of the communal bed, my parents were already making coffee. I heard my mother say, "Ed, look at the tent. Something tried to get in." The unfinished pot of food was tucked inside the door which was secured for the night. Claw marks scored the canvas where the pot was stored.

The days were sunny and warm. We were our playmates and explored and rambled in the woods and by the river. When our parents called us for lunch, I saw something furry in the tall grass. As I approached, a rabbit looked up from the flower it was munching. I stepped quietly toward it until I was within a hand's reach and squatted down in front of it. The bunny continued eating, watching me. There we sat for some minutes, studying each other, until a rowdy brother ran up to re-announce that lunch was ready.

Later that evening, our father beckoned us with a soft voice and a gesture of his hand. He held his camera in the other. He was nose-to-nose with a squirrel sitting on a pine branch just behind the tent. Like the rabbit, the animal was more interested in eating a green pinecone than in our presence. We watched bits of green and white cone scatter as he skillfully ate whatever part squirrels eat.

Several nights later, as my brothers poked at coals in the fire ring, the "Old Man of the Mountain" walked into our camp and asked to heat water on the fire. David immediately brightened and took a seat on the ground right by him.

"Of course," my father said, inviting him in. "Can I offer you something to eat? We have beans and frankfurters left."

The stranger declined, stating he was "orthodox," a word I had never heard before. My father nodded his head, and they began one of those adult conversations that I could only follow in bits about God, the chosen people, and Jesus. My brothers and I watched, open-mouthed, as he made his tea with water he boiled in a tin can and poured molasses over saltines. Sometimes, the syrup dripped onto his grey-white beard. The glow of the fire on the faces of the grown men made them seem timeless and ethereal. As my younger siblings' heads began to nod, Mom gathered us all into bed, while the discussion continued around the campfire. The next day the old man was gone.

Early one morning, as my brothers and mother slept, I joined my father at the campfire. He had already boiled water for our morning hot chocolate and oatmeal. He was reading a book that had the picture of an older man with disheveled white hair and a quiet grin on the cover. He put it down as I approached and showed me his coffee cup.

"See this coffee, Joanne? You and it are traveling at hundreds of thousands of miles an hour." That phrase was my introduction to Einstein's theory of relativity.

I heard the river chuckle, tickling the banks. A breeze ran its hand across the tall green grass, then up to ruffle the tops of the trees. Near the tent, a branch shuddered and a squirrel ran down it to grab an immature pinecone. Birds pecked for crumbs under the picnic table. Everything was traveling.

When my brothers and I collectively smelled worse than the mustiness of the tent, my father marched us all down to the river. The water was still as cold as the melted snow that formed it. We pleaded and begged Dad not to dip us in the water, although we were daily playing in it. We each got a Navy bath — dunk, soap, dunk — and ran back to the constant campfire. On Sunday, my father conducted a church service, part in Latin, most in English, to fulfill the Mass obligation.

There were no trash cans at the campsite. Every few days, my mother drove us to the designated garbage dump. My older two brothers and I had the duty of tossing the bags of trash out the station wagon's back window. One day, to our delight, three large black bears were foraging in the dump for leftovers. We watched transfixed at being so close to animals larger than we were.

"Are you done yet?" my mother asked from the driver's seat. When we did not answer immediately, she turned to see what occupied us and spotted one of the beasts just feet from the car. It was the only time anyone had ever done a wheelie in a `60 Chevy station wagon.

By the time we ended our vacation, we were sun-kissed, tow-headed, feral children who loved camping. Reluctantly, we packed for the journey home. Traveling down the gravel road, my brothers and I searched the countryside for the "Old Man of the Mountain."

Chocolate Monopoly
(a poem)
Gail Smith Langley

In the hot Alabama summers of our childhood,
Marybeth and I would spend the unending days,
Installed on her screen porch, under the humming,
    belt-and-pulley fan.
Prone on our bellies, chilled by slate tiles,
heads propped like music scores,
We peered from opponent sides of a Monopoly board,
Soberly studying Marvin Gardens, Reading Railroad,
    Water Works, and Chance.

The nourishment for our arduous efforts in the world
    of real estate,
A simple provision, one to a girl, a milk chocolate Hershey bar,
Machine pressed into twelve precise portions
    for rationing at our leisure.
Resting on her laurels, my worthy opponent would only remove
    the silver-brown wrapper
After acquiring a prime property, Boardwalk or Park Place.
By this time, I had consumed three squares
    of my confectionary.

As the day drifted on, my adversary had reserved
    a lion's share of her treat.
While I tried to restrain my desire for my mouth-melting bits.
Marybeth delighted in charging rent on acquired properties
All the while relishing her smug moderation and self-restraint.

In the late afternoon, as I struggled to save
      the last cocoa portion,
In chocolate desire, I lost all concentration
      on the game at hand.

Not once did my delectable squares survive the lengthy parlay.
Usually the day ran its course with no clear cartel victory,
Yet there was the triumph of Marybeth's moral fiber.
Even as a young girl, I became aware of a fault in my character.
Waving goodbye, Marybeth savored her last chocolate square
As I walked the block home in a cloud of gluttony.

Just another kind of game, one that took years to master.
A solution, better than drawing a *Get out of Jail Free* card.
Better than owning a monopoly of railroads, or passing *Go*,
Is knowing the secret to winning, a spare chocolate bar
      in my pocket.

Mid-century Man and a Mule Named William
Gail Smith Langley

A Black man named Bruce and a mule named William
Travel by buckboard down my street on Saturdays.
My road is a straight shot to the A&P where they are headed.
If Bruce and William are having a traveling slow day,
We, the neighboring children, trot by the wagon
      begging for a ride.
Most times, the old man and the mule ignore the congregation.
Yet, on rare occasion, the buckboard comes to a halt.
"If you gets on, you be walking back," states the man Bruce.
We clamber aboard in happy acceptance of the contract.
It is then, Bruce, a singular man, speaks to us in tongues.
Mesmerized and enchanted, we become remarkably stilled.
This unexplained marvel of language we take in stride.

That century now turned, I am as old as the man in memory.
In reminiscence, I remain puzzled by the curious verse.
Rudiments of a lost dialect? A charismatic spiritual?
Was Bruce bamboozling the brood for his amusement?
While the mystery of the spoken words goes unanswered,
I will hold the prose in my keeping as an ancient blessing.
So worth the long walk home from the A&P.

Chapter 2
Teenage Mutants

It Looks Like I Made It
Katie Lamar Jackson

Perfection was my grandmother's brand. Her kitchen, library, garden, pantry, deep freeze, and sewing room were always in flawless order. Anything she created in those rooms, from dinner to historic treatises for her Daughters of the American Revolution chapter, were impeccably prepared.

For example, the school dresses and play outfits she made for my sister and me were so precisely cut and stitched that everyone thought they were store-bought, which was a great compliment in those days.

In her home, dust never stayed on a surface longer than a day, silver never tarnished, china plates never chipped, beds were never left unmade. The books in her library, which included social and biblical histories, the classics (*Ulysses* and *The Odyssey* to *Leaves of Grass* and *Little Women*), and a smattering of titles by such Mystics as Edgar Cayce and Juno Kayy Walton — my grandmother believed in a Methodist God but had a superstitious soul — were labeled and arranged on the Dewey Decimal system.

She never left the house, even to go to the local A&P or to drop off a casserole to an ailing neighbor, without donning an immaculately pressed dress (I never saw her in pants except pajama bottoms), fluffing and then immobilizing her coif with aerosol hairspray, and dusting her ample décolletage with powder, usually Jungle Gardenia.

She tried to teach me how to make and do things flawlessly, and by the book (as in Emily Post's treatise on everyday etiquette). But she failed, maybe the only failure of her life.

I remember when she tried to teach me to sew. We ironed the pattern, then the fabric, turning it round and round until we found its true bias grain. We cut and pinned it with precision, sewed it together on her Singer, and made buttonholes and hems by hand. Then I tried it on.

"It looks like you made it," she said. "But it will do for a first try."

I don't think she meant it as a criticism. She was not unkind, just uncompromising. But I never sewed again and almost everything I and my hands have made since has felt imperfect, at least when I judge them by her standards, which throw shade on my own. My layer cakes lean precariously to one side, my hair is a fly-away mess, my clothes are unstarched, my tabletops dusty. My life looks like I made it, which I have. But it will do for a first try.

Pepper's Secret
Mary Dansak

All I wanted to do was ride horses, all day, every day, forever and ever, amen, but my parents refused to get me a horse. Instead, they signed me up for weekly horseback riding lessons. I loved Thursdays, even when Mrs. Butterworth made us practice serpentines and figure eights endlessly, even on rainy days when we cleaned stalls and oiled tack. There was one thing I didn't love about horseback riding lessons, and that was competing in the horse shows.

Mrs. Butterworth insisted we compete. When Mrs. Peacock, my piano teacher, made me perform in my second recital (I froze completely in my first, never making it past one note of a stupid song I thought I'd memorized), I refused to take another piano lesson. Giving up horseback riding, however, was not an option.

It wasn't just that I had stage fright, I was also noncompetitive. Still am. I don't care who wins. Not only that, I was embarrassed about my riding boots. My calves, a maternal inheritance now the envy of musclemen, were too big for real riding boots and I had to wear black plastic rain boots from Sears and Roebuck. Oh, and my mother made my jacket. It was red. I stood out like a sore thumb against the other young riders, all put-together with their blue jackets, tan breeches, and real leather riding boots.

If all that wasn't bad enough, my brother, who didn't really love horses but took lessons for the heck of it, beat me in the last horse show I rode in. Radically physical, a magician of coordination and strength, he didn't even seem to care that he got the first-place ribbon, while I, the hard-working, dedicated, horse-loving sister took home the second-place ribbon, my glossy red ribbon of shame.

And so, as the end-of-the-year show date approached, I was full of angst and dread. The only silver lining was that this year I was doing a jumping course. I loved jumping. Left to my own devices, I'd forgo the saddle and jump bareback. Still, the thought of competitive jumping made my stomach knot up and my eyes sting with tears.

I was assigned to ride Pepper, a broad-backed white horse with soulful, dark eyes. He had a thick mane and a muscular neck. Pepper was a little on the stocky side, and he and I did not have a groove. I dreaded the horse show even more.

Pepper and I had work to do. We practiced for weeks. I wanted the course seared into my head: start with the cross rail on the left side of the ring. Then over to the verticals, circle back and swing to the wall. We'd end with a combination. Pepper had to push to make the three jumps with only one stride in between. I leaned into him with every jump and told him he was a fine, fine boy. I worried about his short legs but never let him know.

I soon realized that Pepper, unlikely though it seemed, enjoyed jumping. He didn't need coaxing even one little bit to take on those higher jumps. Riding Pepper week after week, working on our signals and language as much as learning the course, I could almost forget there was a show coming up.

Like a fast awakening from a pleasant dream, the day of horse show arrived. My mother insisted on taking pictures of us. My thin dishwater-blonde hair, pulled back into a little net at the nape of my neck, threatened to slip out from under my hard hat. I was a scrappy, sweaty kid, no glamour. My brother grinned from ear to ear, unfazed by the show, unfazed by anything. As soon as she snapped the picture, I mounted Pepper and we headed for the gate. My mother smiled and waved. My brother stuck out his tongue. I felt my mouth and throat go dry.

Pepper stomped his foot in anticipation of our turn. "Stop," I whispered. The judges would not look kindly on this antsy behavior. In response, Pepper switched his tightly braided tail repeatedly.

And then it was our turn. Just as I had done in my debacle of a piano recital, I froze. My mind emptied completely. What was the course? Where should we start? One second seemed to drag into an hour as I stared at the rails and barrels in confusion. If only a huge hole would open up and swallow us! I fought back tears.

Pepper waited for his cue, finally taking matters into his own hooves. Head held high, he entered the ring. He broke into a gentle canter, then began the course, taking every turn perfectly, gliding over every jump effortlessly. I was nothing more than a passenger with no idea of our destination. It was all over in a flash, and then everyone clapped. Pepper tossed his head as if trying to shake his mane loose of its silly button braids. I smiled nervously.

We won first place in that event. I got a big blue ribbon that I did not deserve. Pepper did it all. If I could've given that ribbon to Pepper I would've, but I didn't want to confess to Mrs. Butterworth that I forgot the course. Instead, I took the ribbon home and hung it on my bookshelf, right next to the red ribbon from the year before. Every time I looked at it, I felt guilty.

Later that year I finally got my own horse, leaving me free to quit riding lessons and horse shows forever. But Karma had the last laugh. My horse was a gaited horse, meaning that instead of trotting he paced, a gait as smooth as silk but one that made jumping difficult without professional training. I gave up jumping along with horse shows.

As for that final horse show, until this day, I'd never told a soul about my ill-gotten gains. Mrs. Butterworth, if you're reading this, I confess that it was Pepper all along.

The Secret Bra
Margee Bright Ragland

September 7, 1962

I am in eighth grade at W.F. Dykes High School in Atlanta, Georgia. My school has students from eighth through twelfth grades, so I am a sub-freshman. High school is so different than elementary school. We change classes and have different teachers. There are so many students.

The seniors resemble adults. The girls have huge breasts, tiny waists, and bouffant hair styles that Marie Antoinette would envy. The boys are muscular football players with giant necks, bulging biceps, and tight butts. I feel so out of place at this school. I am skinny and flat-chested with thin dark hair and cat-eye glasses. There are no signs that my breasts will start to grow. I haven't even had a period. Currently, I'm devising a plan for my transformation to beauty and acceptance.

September 9, 1962

The padded bra I saw today at Woolworths was calling my name. It was a B cup made of rigid material, so the bra stuck out to nice cone points. I tried it on, and of course, my flat chest just rested behind the air-filled cups. These cups are very firm, so I won't have to stuff socks into them. I'll just put it on and wow, bosoms!

My mother refused to buy me that bra. She argued that my triple-A training bra was just fine, and when my boobs grew, we would see about another bra.

September 28, 1962

I've been saving my coins and finally have enough to buy that bra. I decided to get the C cup and really make a statement. Of course, I will have to hide it in my book bag and put it on in the restroom when I get to school. Cannot wait to wear it next week. I should wear a sweater.

October 3, 1962

This is my first day wearing my new bra. It doesn't fit that well under my shirt. I'm getting used to wearing it before I wear a tight sweater. I pulled the cups up kind of high for maximum effect. It's like my breasts are growing directly out of my collar bones, but I think I look good. Got some glances from some ninth-grade boys who had never noticed me before. I'm getting up my nerve to hang around some guys during lunch. Wish me luck. I've also stopped wearing my glasses between classes and at lunch. It's a little hard to see what's happening at a distance, but I can see pretty well up close.

October 10, 1962

Have I ever mentioned how much a detest Nancy Thompson? I will hate her forever. It's difficult for me to even record the vile act she inflicted on me during lunch today. One day I may look back on today and laugh, but I doubt it.

So, I was chatting with some real friends, edging toward the table where the football players were sitting. I had on my cream-colored pullover sweater and was kind of sticking out my chest for maximum effect. Out of nowhere, Nancy appeared and walked toward me. She extended her index fingers and poked me directly in the center of each of my C cups. My fake bosoms indented dramatically and remained in that position for several seconds until they suddenly popped back into shape. "Nice boobs, Margee," said that evil witch. Everyone in the vicinity burst into laughter.

    I quickly got the hell out of the lunchroom and ran to the restroom. My face was bright red, like the worst sunburn of my life. I headed for a stall and removed that stupid bra. I hated that bra. I hated Nancy Thompson, and I hated myself for being such a fool. I threw the bra in the trash can and headed for my next class. In a Clark Kent move, I put my glasses on hoping no one in my class would recognize me as the same humiliated girl in the lunchroom.

October 24, 1962
    It's been several weeks since the bra incident. I've gone back to my training bra. I've started wearing cardigan sweaters over my button-down collar shirts to create a sense of mystery. My mother bought me a baby blue Bobbie Brooks matching shirt, skirt, and sweater combo. I'm feeling pretty sharp.

November 14, 1962
    Judy Swaim, my best friend, and I have purchased wide leather belts in several colors that we can tighten to make our waists look really small. Judy is extremely petite, so she can cinch up her belt creating a Scarlet O'Hara waist. I am giving myself a stomachache. My mother told me I was ruining my intestines. Why is beauty so painful?

That February
Mary Dansak

Jenny Bea and I warmed our frozen fingers over a steaming pile of freshly laid horse manure. We were crammed into one stall with two horses. Through the cracks in the crudely built wooden walls, the brilliant and cold February sunshine streamed in thin lines, illuminating the steam rising off the horses' bodies. There were no thoughts about getting kicked or bitten in these close quarters, only thoughts of keeping the freezing cold at bay.

"Let's groom them," I said, thinking the movement would warm our fingers. The horses stood still, enjoying the curry combs and brushes. They seemed oblivious to the cold, despite the condensation puffing out of their nostrils.

My horse, Colti, rubbed his huge red head against my torso. He was the best horse in the world. He was big, he was strong, he was wild, and he was affectionate. He was also mine. Mine, mine, mine! I hugged his head close to me while I brushed out his cream-colored forelock. I could feel his hard skull pressing against my ribs. People think horses' hooves are the dangerous body parts, but a horse's skull is a weapon, I thought, remembering times when I'd taken a head-butt to the chin. Colti would never head-butt me. He was an enormous, gentle boy.

My riding teacher taught us to tidy up horses' manes by grasping the longest strands and pushing the surrounding mane up and away, twirling the long offenders around our fingers, and yanking like all get out. "It doesn't hurt," she assured us. I'd pull so hard the skin of the horse's whole neck would move. "Pull!" she'd say, and finally the strand of long, course mane would come loose. I'd flick it away for the rats and birds to build nests with.

"Never cut the mane. Pull it out! And even if you like it long, never let it go past the neck." She tried to convince us that a horse's mane hanging down past its neck was sloppy and unseemly.

Well, that was all good and fine for her, but Colti was my horse. I let his mane grow longer than his neck. I braided flowers into it, twirled it, brushed it out, washed it, groomed him to be a fine, fine prince of a boy. He was my best friend.

Now I put my hands up under his long, wild mane and let my fingers bask in the warmth of his neck.

"Do you think they'll come soon?" Jenny Bea asked, teeth chattering. My dad and stepmom were due to fetch us any minute.

"I hope so," I said. It was almost dark.

Finally, the yellow Toyota truck pulled up to the barn. I threw my arms around Colti and kissed him a thousand times, then opened the door to the stall so the horses could come and go as they pleased, into the paddocks and pastures beyond. As always, he followed me to the gate and watched me walk away. Then he nickered, making that breathy, gravelly sound in his throat, a friendly message, one of my favorite noises of all time. This meant I had to go back for another hug, and another. I had a nickering horse. I was the luckiest girl in the world.

It was that February, the one with the warming horse manure and the mornings of going to the barn early to break the ice on the water bin, that Colti died. There was cruelty involved, and madness, and selfishness on the part of someone else who had horses at that barn, and who, unlike my careful thirteen-year-old self, did not leave the doors open for horses to come and go, but instead locked Colti out of the barn, away from his hay, in a small corral where Colti gnawed the bark completely off a Chinaberry tree. This led to colic and, despite Herculean efforts from the doctors at the university vet school, death.

About a week after my horse died and my life as I knew it ended, I picked up a packet of photos. I thumbed through pictures of my friends, my dog, and then stopped short. There was Colti, his gorgeous red coat gleaming, his long, cream-colored mane emanating golden light against a cold February sky, nickering for me to come back one more time.

Firetruck
Joanne Camp

Not all Catholic schools had the sour-faced, knuckle-wrapping nuns that fill the memories of so many former students. After my northern Catholic school experience, the nuns at St. Paul the Apostle in South Carolina were quite benevolent. They wore long black robes and veils like so many of the religious sisters of the time, but their attitudes were more modern. They smiled, joked, and were ready to give a hug to any child who needed it.

After most of the children left for the day, Sister Claire Marie and Sister Mary Clare would put on their Converse sneakers, black of course, and pair off in a rollicking game of pick-up basketball, veils flying like dreadlocks. The Alexander children were witnesses to several of these games as my mother, tending to smaller preschool children, was often late to pick us up. Despite their modern ways, the sisters still proselytized all the girls to the religious life, and all the boys into the priesthood.

To this means, the girls in the ninth grade, the highest grade in the school, were invited to the inner sanctum of the convent to see how the nuns lived. We saw the sisters sitting around the gathering room, without their veils. They had hair, although it was cut short for convenience. We helped cut the wimples and headbands from sheets of plastic and saw the particular way their rope belts were tied to accommodate the dangling rosary. It was very romantic and mystical, and in my daydreams, I pictured myself clad in black flowing robes, piously clutching a rosary.

Outside St. Paul the Apostle school, it was the mid-`60s, the era of rock and roll, not Gregorian chant, and miniskirts, not floor-length habits. We Catholic girls wore pleated plaid skirts with hems that touched the floor when we knelt, white blouses buttoned to the neck, and red blazers. Some girls would roll their waistbands up until their hem reached mid-thigh, then button their blazers over the wad, before strolling downtown. I did not. These girls had 45 speed records of the Beatles, the Monkees, and Strawberry Alarm Clock. I did not. These girls would sneak into the movies to watch *James Bond* or *Barbarella*, both condemned by the Legion of Decency. I did not.

The Beatles declared themselves greater than Jesus; they were not played in my house. I did watch the Monkees weekly on T.V. as they were just harmless fools who sang. I was not aware that there was a Strawberry Alarm Clock. And if the Legion of Decency said you could not watch a movie, I did not. I kept my nose in books. Charles Dickens, Emily Bronte, and Madeline L'Engle gave me all the information I needed.

My favorite hangout was the school library, and I reveled in the Dewey Decimal system. One of the great joys of my last year at St. Paul's was working in the library — a privilege given to the older girls who volunteered, which all seven girls in the ninth grade did. There we worked at our ease, talking and visiting unsupervised as we replaced the books returned by the children from the lower grades. Our duties were to check those books dumped on the return dolly for damage, and gently restore them to their proper shelf and place. The library contained twenty parallel shelves of books, a librarian's desk, and a free-standing tiltable blackboard, that was green.

One day, as we were putting up the books, three of the girls — Carol, Debbie, and Donna — huddled gossiping and giggling. Carol was tall, with a stylish Twiggy haircut. Forward and brave, she talked with boys from our class during recess. Debbie was petite and slender. She had straight auburn brown hair that almost reached her waist. She kept it pulled back with a tortoise-shell hair band. She and Donna hiked up their skirts before leaving campus and strolled downtown in search of the latest fashions. When we were supposed to be researching a term paper in the library, I saw Debbie share her favorite Bobby Brooks look from a copy of *Seventeen* magazine with Donna. Donna's hair was cut in a shoulder-length page-boy. At the beginning of the school year, she was sent home because she had painted her nails fiery red.

Except for my uniform, I sewed my clothes at home. My dishwater-blonde hair was wavy, although I sometimes rolled it with empty orange juice cans to straighten it. My hairstylist was my mother whose attempt at cutting bangs always left them too short. I wore thick glasses to cure my near-sightedness. I was very short, and when the girls in the class started blossoming, I remained flat-chested. I looked more like a twelve-year-old than my fifteen years.

I heard Carol question the group, "What begins with F and ends with U-C-K?"

Always loving a riddle, I picked up a piece of chalk on the blackboard and wrote an exact block F, then a space and U, C, and K in all capital letters on the green blackboard. I stood back and pushed my thick, light-blue framed glasses up on my nose, pondering the answer. Carol noticed the blackboard and smirked. We heard the click of sensible shoes in the hall and

Sister Walburga, the principal and disciplinarian, opened the door. Carol's face went white, and she darted to the board. Erasing my letters, she hissed "'firetruck,' the answer is 'firetruck.'"

Winged Feet of Mercury
Marian Carcache

Literary scholars are not in agreement on whether John Cleland intended Fanny Hill's name to be a play on "Mound of Venus," but there was not much discussion about it around Jernigan in 1966 when I was stealthily reading *Memoirs of a Woman of Pleasure* (1748) while leaning over the recipe drawer in the kitchen where it was hidden.

One of our neighbors lent the book to Mama who read every afternoon between fixing dinner and fixing supper. I remember being jealous as a child of the Bronte sisters, Daphne Du Maurier, Phyllis Whitney, and Mary Stewart. After only a few pages, Mama pronounced Fanny Hill as "vulgar," and into the recipe drawer it went until she could return it to its owner. She certainly didn't want it out in plain view in case company dropped in. Mama, whose house was spotless to a fault, was not a fan of "trash" of any kind.

One afternoon, on my way to make Jewel Cookies — a delicious recipe from my *Junior Cookbook* that included flour, butter, sugar, vanilla flavoring, and chopped-up colorful gumdrops — I discovered the erotic masterpiece, quite the "jewel" itself.

As my professor of Eighteenth-Century literature at Auburn pointed out decades later, there is not one "dirty" word in this novel, but it is one of the most banned books in history. Cleland took delight in playing with language when referring to body parts. I dare say that his clever phrases such as "cloven spot," "mighty machine," and "all-delicious twin orbs" would escape even Zuckerberg's sneaky little algorithm.

Lest I get caught reading the erotic masterpiece — or what Mama had deemed "filth" — I became quite adept at watching the zinnia-lined brick path to the back door while reading about Fanny's adventures. If I caught sight of Mama coming down the walkway, I would slam the drawer shut and, faster than quicksilver, make it back to the kitchen table where my Nifty Space-Saver magnetic binder and schoolbooks lay open.

So went the second age of this Mystic — the schoolgirl who jumped from the adventures of Sally, Dick, and Jane to those of Fanny and Charles in jig time.

Chapter 3
Enlightenment and Erudition

Cool Kid Rising
Mary Dansak

My stepmother Janie drove a cream-colored Firebird complete with the giant Phoenix on the hood. I'd been raised to call that tacky, and my reaction to that spread-Eagle bird with the sideways head is still in me. Tacky! Janie is from a good Tennessee family. Her dad was a doctor. I still can't believe she had the Phoenix on the hood. Wait, maybe she didn't have the Phoenix on the hood and I'm just inventing it to make my story cooler. Come to think of it, I really don't know. But she definitely had a cream-colored Firebird. I could feel the engine in that car. It felt different than the engines in the Volkswagens and the Fords I'd been toted around in. She let me drive it all the time, that is, with her beside me. I only had a learner's permit. Tacky or not, I have to admit I did feel a little bit cool driving that car.

Now, let's establish one thing: I was not a cool kid. I wanted to be a cool kid. I hung out with a number of cool kids. The coolest kids of all were the boys who got together downtown on Sundays and played jazz. I didn't even like the music, but I'd go to their jam sessions with my girlfriends and feign clove-scented interest. My girlfriends were prettier and skinnier than I was, and, I'll be honest, cooler. They got much more attention from the cool boys, who plucked their instruments and tapped their toes, cigarettes hanging from their mouths, sipping bourbon on ice between riffs and solos. Occasionally, I got a smile. If I was really mooning, I got a wink.

One weekend my dad and Janie went out of town. Robert and I were seventeen and fifteen, old enough to stay home alone. I'm sure Janie and my dad had given up so completely with Robert that the worst-case scenario, he'd end up in jail, didn't sound so bad. And they didn't have to worry about me because I was good.

I was good, but I wanted to be cool and here was my chance. What if I just drove myself downtown to the jam session in the Firebird? My heart pitter-pattered at the thought, and I quickly made up my mind. The keys to the Firebird hung by the door, as innocent as an ice cream cone, no clue that they were about to be snatched up and used in an illegal act. Now my heart pounded, and my knees went weak, but I did it. I grabbed those keys, took the porch steps two at a time, and flung myself into that car like it was my own.

I lit a cigarette, Marlboro Light (I'd long graduated from Virginia Slim Menthol Lights), not to calm my nerves but to enhance my image. If I got caught doing this, I'd be in so much trouble. I could be arrested, right? Driving at age fifteen with no license? My stepmother would probably get in trouble too for leaving the keys, those loaded weapons, around so casually. And if I got in an accident, well, I just couldn't even imagine how bad it would be. So I drove like a grandma, eyes glued to the road, hands gripping the wheel at ten-and-two, completely forgetting about the way the cool kids drive with their wrists draped over the wheel. With tremendous relief, I pulled into a parking place downtown without incident.

I stepped out of the car. I didn't get in a wreck! That wasn't so bad. Still, I was shaking like a leaf. I calmed myself enough to go into the building where the guys were jamming and smoking and drinking and thinking about two million and one things which did not include me or how I got downtown or even whether or not I was old enough to drive.

Where were my girlfriends? They were nowhere to be seen. Being there without them was awkward, stiff, and made me feel stupid. What was I doing here?

I left the jam session quickly. No one saw my exit. No one saw me get into the cream-colored Firebird with or without the Phoenix on the hood, light a cigarette, look over my shoulder with a very Mary Tyler Moore head toss, and back out onto the street. When I got home, I slipped the keys right back onto the key hook by the door and went into my bedroom to sit on my bed, listen to "The Secret Life of Plants" on my Sears stereo, and write very bad poetry in my journal.

The next evening, around dinner time, Janie got a call from a friend. To this day I don't know if the friend was like, "Oh I saw your car downtown this weekend. Started to stop by and say hi, but you know, I was in such a hurry," or "Hey, I know you were out of town this weekend, so I just wanted to let you know that your car was out joyriding without you."

"Robert, get in here!" Janie yelled, slamming the phone into the receiver. She immediately began berating Robert for driving her car downtown.

"Why would I take your car? I have my own car!" Robert yelled back. Those two could really go at it. It was true, though; he did have his own car. Granted, Robert's car didn't have fenders or a windshield, and the hood was held down with a bungee cord, and he used a fingernail file for a key, but he didn't need the Firebird to be cool. He just was cool.

Suddenly the room was silent. I wonder just how red my face grew. Robert took one look at me and burst into the most genuine peal of laughter. He threw his head back and roared. "I didn't take the car," he gasped between guffaws, "she did!" He pointed at me, and I thought he was going to wet his pants. I thought I was going to wet my pants too, but for different reasons.

I got in trouble, grounded for a long, long time. But something more important happened in that moment with Robert pointing at me laughing; my father's face, also with a cigarette dangling from his lips (Vantage), drawn up into incredulous scorn; my stepmother's fury paused just long enough to recover from the shock of me, the good one, doing this deed.

I cried and ran from the room. I holed up once again in my bedroom with a pen and a notebook. I wrote and wrote about what I had done. I wrote and I cried and I didn't feel one drop of remorse. Instead, I was mad. Mad that I had done something so stupid to get the attention of a bunch of dudes who didn't give one flying fuck about me; mad that it was so astonishing that I, a goody-goody two shoes, was capable of being bad; mad that I wasn't cool; mad that I wanted to be cool; mad that nobody understood me nor would they ever, ever, ever, ever understand me and I was destined to live in my isolated, un cool, misunderstood brain forever.

One week later, I walked into the kitchen where my dad, stepmother, and brother were having coffee (Folgers Crystals, with water heated in a Hot Pot). They were all going about their morning over pancakes and the Sunday funnies, making plans which did not include me because I was grounded.

I cleared my throat. "I have something to say," I said, not shaking or crying and also not caring.

"I've been good all my life. And he's been bad all his life." I pointed at Robert who looked up at me for the first time. "And it hasn't done me any good. I have the same rules as he does. I have the same curfew as he does. I don't have one single privilege he doesn't have."

I paused. Both my dad and Janie were listening. Robert had turned back to the Sunday funnies.

"I just want to let you know that I'm not going to be good anymore."

There was no response.

I made my own cup of instant coffee and calmly went back to my room to write more bad poetry about the moon, unicorns, fairies, gnomes, and the tragic failures of all mankind.

Riding with the Boss
Mary Dansak

After two years of college in my hometown, I transferred to the University of Massachusetts-Boston, a commuter school on a spit of land in a harbor in the town of Dorchester. I didn't have a car, and despite my hour-long daily commute, I fell soundly in love with public transportation.

About this time, I purchased a Walkman, a fancy gadget for playing cassette tapes which magically filled springy metal headphones with tunes. This purchase was totally out of character. I was low tech and like all good college students, I was Ramen Noodle poor. I didn't have a television, an answering machine, a toaster oven, or any kind of stereo, so this Walkman felt like a grand extravagance. The small collection of cassette tapes I owned largely came from the Columbia Record and Tape Club, where you could get eleven cassettes for a penny with the promise to buy one a month at full price after that. I joined several times and broke every contract.

One afternoon, I got *Born in the USA* in the mail. I decided I'd give it a good first listen on a city bus. God, I loved those buses. My mama told me that the buses were actually free for the price of our tax dollars, and the fifty-cent fare was just for people who had it. Sure enough, once when I didn't have a dime to my name and wanted to get on the bus to get out of the rain, I told the driver I didn't have the fare and he waved me onboard.

Riding through the neighborhoods in the city and beyond, the Boss singing directly into my very own ears, I experienced a melancholia I'd never met before. He made me nostalgic for a place I'd never known and filled me with a tragic fear of being stuck forever in that unknown place I was nostalgic for at the same time that I feared it.

What was this exactly, and why, now, was that kid on the sidewalk we just passed so haunting? What had I done with my own teenage dreams, and were they heavy like this, and did they need to be sung and cemented into anthems?

Streets rolled by. Neighborhoods rolled by. People of all stripes got on and off the bus, and I leaned against the window and listened to tunes, awash in a confusing blend of angst and love for humanity.

After that day, I made a habit of riding with the Boss.

Those aimless bus rides were a luxury in my busy life of college, waiting tables, and studying. But I couldn't stop myself. I was chasing an ephemeral vision of some parallel life, and for just this one brief moment, I had the freedom to chase it on my own, with no one looking for me, needing me, or calling out my name.

One day I was jolted out of my reverie when the bus stopped in a parking lot full of other buses. The bus driver turned around and yelled at me that I'd come to the end of the line, and I had to get off the bus. I nodded and headed out into what immediately struck me as a bus graveyard, with the buses parked in rows, all their blinking lights shut down. I walked out of the lot through a chain link gate and into a neighborhood I'd never seen before. A day had become a night.

I don't even remember how I got home. I only remember that one night I rode a bus to the end of the line with the Boss singing to me about the wind in my hair and I didn't have to answer to a soul.

Spring Break Cruise in Haiku
Margee Bright Ragland

Spring Break, Nassau Cruise
Four wild girls looking for fun
Partying like rock stars

Caribbean blue salt seas
Pristine white sand beaches awaiting
Hot sun and cold drinks

Ship's bar open twenty-four seven
Our bartender is named Alfie
What is it all about?

D-deck has tiny rooms
Our bunks stacked like submarine beds
Must hang out on deck

Our key opens all doors
Nancy finds bourbon, Leslye boxer shorts
D-deck looted by our crew

Swimming with the fishes
Our island destination reached
Sun, swim, drink, repeat

Returning to our ship
Evenings singing and dancing with the band
Under a star-filled sky.

Docking in Miami
Glowing tans and throbbing heads
Auburn, we're returning.

Tornado
Joanne Camp

"Dad, call Joanne. Call Jimmy." Sixteen-year-old Mark was insistent. He had had a bad dream. As my brothers and sisters mingled around getting breakfast, Mark persistently asked my father to check on me and my brother. Dad was reading the morning paper standing with his back to the kitchen sink and drinking his first cup of coffee. This was the third time Mark made this plea. Finally, my father put his cup down and went to the phone booth which was tucked in the corner of the main L-shaped hallway of the house. The phone booth was a cast-off from the telephone company and housed the children's phone. It was decorated with graffiti and friends' phone numbers.

"The line's busy," He called back to the kitchen.

"Go, check on them, Dad."

***

After Mary, my first college roommate decided to return north to join her parents, I had to find another place to live. She and I had shared an apartment about two blocks from the police department and about six blocks from Auburn University, where we both attended school.

When she left, my father decided that I needed to become more fiscally responsible. I was already paying my rent, utilities, books, and tuition. I had paid off my car, at my father's insistence, before moving out of my parent's house. And I worked part-time and carried a full load at college. He thought I needed to invest in a home.

Home ownership to a college student meant a single-wide trailer. I found a used one in Conway's trailer park on Highway

14, which was inhabited by students who could not afford to live in the established trailer parks closer to the university or the pricey apartments near campus. The mobile home had two bedrooms, one at each end. Both rooms had a bathroom. In the center was a kitchen with an eating nook. The adjacent living area was separated from the kitchen by a half wall. There was a front door in the living area and a backdoor in the kitchen. The siding on the outside of the trailer was a faded mustard-yellow; the paneling on the inside was dark fake wood.

 Conway's trailer park was isolated from the town, established in an old pecan orchard. Many of the ancient trees still loomed over the homes tucked in between the rows. It was full of students like me who worked and studied their way through college. Mr. Conway, a tall, lean Southern gentleman, appreciated his clientele. So long as there were no loud parties, no fights, and you paid your lot rent regularly, he was an affable landlord. Residents were invited to fish the ponds at the back of the park and gather what few pecans the old trees produced. Mr. Conway would regularly stroll through the park to chat or offer advice or lend tools for minor repairs.

 My next youngest brother, Jimmy, had just enrolled in college so it was decreed that he would reside with me. We had lived together for eighteen years, so that did not seem a hardship. He was only eleven months younger than I was. We shared the same blond hair, fair skin, and freckles. His hair was almost as long as mine. Jimmy was a physics major; I was in language. We had separate class schedules, and our schools were across campus from each other. We had different friends. His were guitar players who enjoyed the music scene in downtown Auburn and Waverly. Mine were linguists and foreign students who hung out at the student center. We rarely saw each other.

The trailer was furnished in standard college-student style. We both absconded with our mattresses and box springs from home. I commandeered the bedroom farthest away from the road as its bathroom was attached and it had a full-length mirror on the back of the door.

I had previously purchased a used brown corduroy sofa, which was our only living room furniture except for a thrift store table and chairs which occupied another corner. We had a radio, but no television. I had my sewing machine set up against the half wall in the kitchen. With the sewing machine, I sewed curtains for the kitchen and living room from J.C. Penney sheets. Home Sweet Trailer.

On the stormy night of spring break in 1974, my brother and I had gone our separate ways. He went to a party with friends in Notasulga and had wisely decided to spend the night there after drinking. I, not so wisely, had fallen asleep at my boyfriend's trailer on Wire Road just a few miles from my own trailer. We realized the weather was bad, but when I arrived at my own home that morning to get ready for work, I saw just how bad.

My single-wide was upside-down barely two feet from my neighbor's. My bedroom was blown out like a firecracker, and insulation hung from the trees like chunky Christmas garland.

As I stood there staring, Mr. Conway strolled up.

"Oh, Joanne, thank God! I came down here to check on you, but I saw that." He pointed to where I had pots of herbs growing on a ledge. The large terra cotta pot of parsley was smashed against the small kitchen window.

"I thought that was your head, so I called the police." As we were talking, my father arrived.

"Where's your brother? Is anyone hurt?" My boyfriend took that as a cue to check on the neighbor. He sidled in between the two trailers and knocked on the door. The door opened about two feet and hit the side of my trailer. The neighbor tried again, hit the trailer, and let out an expletive.

"What the ..." He grabbed his sleep-tousled hair with both hands. His fatigue fog vanished as he became acutely awake. He let out a louder expletive. His trailer was untouched. Looking around, I saw no other homes with the same damage as mine in the nearby area. Across the gravel road, the storm moved a trailer slightly off the blocks that held it level, but it was still upright.

I climbed up over the top of the front door with the help of my father to investigate inside. As the smashed planter hinted, dishes and glasses were broken on the ceiling, which was now the floor. My metal sewing machine was still intact, but as I placed my hand on the half wall to steady myself, I saw a metal sewing bobbin half buried in the post. I wobbled down the hallway to my bedroom. The door was open; the bed was at my feet. I lifted the mattress. Large shards of the mirror from the back of the door gouged into the bed.

Jimmy and I scavenged what few clothes, furniture, and items we could in the following days. We both moved home, but a sister had already claimed my small closed-in porch bedroom, and I slept on the couch.

A few days later, my father called me to his office. When I entered a suited gentleman was seated in one of the visitors' chairs chatting with my father.

"This is the insurance adjuster," my father explained as I sat in the other chair. The man opened his briefcase and began gathering papers.

"So, Miss Alexander," he began, "you pushed over your trailer with a bulldozer, and expect the insurance company to pay you for it?" My mouth dropped and I stared at the adjuster until he and my father started laughing. After a short conversation about what I had lost, he asked me to make a list of all the personal property that was destroyed. Within weeks, I had a check for more money than I had ever had in one lump sum.

As a fiscally responsible adult, I took the money and put a down payment on a summer study program in Spain.

Spain, 1974
Joanne Camp

A water balloon splatted at our feet. Although it was almost nine o'clock at night, the sun was just setting below the horizon. We were sitting on the patio in front of the dormitory sipping Spanish beer.

"Son of a bitch," Maryse yelled and jumped up from her seat. Her soft pink dress was wet at the frilly hem. She was almost six feet tall and had a curvy figure that belied her power.

Sarah looked up and cocked her glass in a toast toward the top of the building five stories up. Sarah was one of the students from Auburn. She had a clear creamy pale complexion. Her light brown hair reached to her shoulders.

"It was Salvador," Sarah said. Maryse jerked her head up to see from where the bomb dropped. Her red frizzy hair joggled with the motion.

"I'm going to kill him!"

"No, no, Maryse, leave them alone. You will only encourage them," I urged in a lazy, calm voice.

Maryse sat and drained her beer. "You can always calm me down."

When the tornadoes of 1974 blew out my mobile home like a firecracker, I was a junior in college. For the past two years, I had been paying some mortgage company for the two-bedroom single-wide. So, when the insurance representative reimbursed me for the totaled trailer, I did what every responsible college student would do — I went to Spain for the summer. I had coveted the study abroad program offered to language majors. But since I was earning my way through college by working part-time during the school year, and full-time during the summer, there was just barely money for tuition, books, room, and board. Most weeks I lived on rice and tea, but always bought cat food for Pyrowacette and Clyde.

This was Auburn's first year to sponsor the Auburn-Alabama Abroad Program, and the administrators had not worked out the kinks. That summer all the participants, male and female, were booked into a male dorm on the University of Madrid campus. Each floor had only one communal bathroom.

This was the post-Woodstock era ("Peace, love and Bobby Sherman") and miniskirts. Co-ed dorms were unheard of, especially in Spain. So, the Spanish occupants of the dorm, mostly rich, wanna-be bullfighters, full of arrogance and swagger, thought the American girls were *"facil"* (easy) and barraged us with a constant chorus of taunts and innuendoes. Most of the female students endured and ignored the cries; some had had enough. On the way to class one day, I found Jill, throwing rocks and screaming at three of the dorm boys who were following her, murmuring veiled obscenities just loud enough for her to hear.

At the dorm, we endured juvenile affronts, like the water balloons, comical attempts to get our response. Some girls swooned at this adolescent attention, but not my two *amigas*. The closest we came to any of the locals was to send our American buddy Bill to learn Spanish curse words from them, which we threw back at the *caballeros* when they tried to bother us.

On weekends we escaped the university, but not the program, by going on excursions to cities and sites on the outskirts of Madrid. Just the weekend before, we visited

Enlightenment and Erudition

Valladolid where I celebrated my twenty-first birthday. The waiters had brought a slice of cake with two small candles melted end to end on the top. They lit the top candle and sang the Spanish version of "Happy Birthday." In his native language, our waiter explained that the top candle symbolized ten years, the bottom candle *diez* (ten), and both candles were *uno*, to represent my new age.

On the outings, a local restaurant provided the main meal, always with a carafe of wine for each table. Many of our fellow students had not traveled abroad and preferred water or Coca-Cola with their meals. Bill, Maryse, Sarah, and I preferred to dine as locals, and there was a constant transfer of carafes from the other tables to the one at which we sat. As a result, our afternoon excursions were animated and spirited.

On this night, we sat on the patio, discussing where we would travel when the program ended within the week. We had fourteen days on our own before the flight back to Atlanta. Bill, our constant escort, although he was Sarah's boyfriend, was going to rent a car. We were heading to the cool of the French-Spanish mountains, the Pyrenees. Bill, the only one in our group taller than Maryse, had joined the program after traveling to parts of France and Italy. He had an open, kind face and his eyes twinkled like a youngster about to commit mischief. He joined us on the patio, but tonight he had an unaccustomed frown on his face.

"What's wrong?" Sarah asked.

"The president is resigning." He replied. I let out a nervous laugh.

"Not funny," Maryse growled at him.

"No. I just heard it on BBC radio," he insisted. "Today at eight o'clock Washington time. Two o'clock in the morning, here."

We stared dumbly at each other. Jose Manuel approached. He was another of the braggarts who liked to come up behind the American girls and pinch them on the butt. He had received a slap in the face from me.

With a cruel grin, he proclaimed in a thick accent, "Yes, your president is resigning; Francisco is on his deathbed. Maybe we kill all the Americans. Who will stop us?" He shrugged as though it was not a big deal.

That night we set our alarms for 1:30 a.m. All the American students met in the common room in the basement where the only television in the dorm was. The low conversations between students stopped as Nixon's familiar face came on the screen at 2:00 a.m. One of the girls was crying softly, as her friend tried to comfort her. The president's words were dubbed in Spanish, and we tried desperately to hear the English over the interpreter's voice. A handful of the Spanish students joined us, but they seemed more interested in the history that was unfolding than in harassing the Americans. None of us slept the rest of the night, and the next morning, we four sat at our usual table in the dining room, hovering over our large cups of café con leche.

"How far is it to the American Embassy?" Maryse asked cutting her eyes to the tables around us.

"Twenty minutes, if you run," Bill replied.

"Should we go to class today?" I asked. Sarah searched for Bill's hand under the table.

"I'm not," Bill replied. "I'm in mourning." Then his mouth turned up at the corners and his eyes narrowed. "Besides, there are only two more classes. Let's start our two weeks early."

I took a long swig of my coffee. "I'll be ready to go in twenty minutes." Maryse's curls bounced up and down with her nod. Sarah squeezed Bill's hand tighter and grinned.

Grad School Confidential
Margee Bright Ragland

July of 1972

Dear Carol,

Sorry I haven't written since I returned from California. My brother, Teddy, and I had quite an adventure traveling across the country together. He was so frightened we would perish in our travels. He even left our parents a farewell note thanking them for being great parents and to pray for him in Heaven.

He only disappeared from me once in Arizona after we had crossed the desert.

While I was taking a much-needed shower he vanished. Searching frantically around our motel, pool, and parking lot, I finally found him two blocks away at a Golden Corral Steak House enjoying a huge T-Bone and baked potato. I forgot that sixteen-year-old boys need to eat often. As long as I made sure he ate three times a day we got along fine the rest of the trip.

Now we're back in Atlanta, safe and sound. I've decided to spend my time seriously pursuing a career in fine art after two years at Technicolor Corporation. I went down to Georgia State University to sign up for a painting course. The counselor looked at my application and said, "You have a BFA. Why don't you apply for our MFA Program."

I replied, "Sure. When do classes begin?"

She sighed. "Well first you have to apply, my dear. You might not be accepted. I'll schedule an interview for you with Mr. Jim Sitton who will evaluate your application and portfolio."

Enlightenment and Erudition

Really Carol, I just wanted to take a painting course. Why was this getting complicated?

Several weeks later
Dear Carol,

My process for acceptance in the MFA program was quite an experience. At 10:00 am on a sunny Tuesday morning, I arrived at Mr. Sitton's office with my application and portfolio. My portfolio consisted of the few paintings I made while we were living in Denver, and I have to admit the paintings were pretty bad. Arranging my work around his office, I could sense Mr. Sitton's displeasure. He had an omnipotent smirk on his very effete face. His manner was slow and deliberate as he moved from painting to painting. I was really uneasy. After all, I just wanted to take a painting course for Christ's sake!

Mr. Sitton finished his tour and then sat behind his desk studying my application. He began holding the application very close to his face and moving his head from side to side. He had very strange mannerisms. I was pretty sure he was going to tell me thank you very much and we'll get back to you, or worse, just ask me to get lost.

Then suddenly he stopped, look directly at me, and asked, "Is this really your birthday?"

I replied, "Yes sir, March 30, 1948."

Sitton: "Do you know anyone else with this birthday?"

Me: "Yes, Vincent Van Gogh." (I am proud that Vincent and I share a birthday).

Sitton: "And do you know anyone else?"

Me: "I know it was the date of the Purchase of Alaska."

Sitton: "I mean other artists?"

Me: "Uh, not right off hand."

Sitton: "March the 30th is the birthday of Francisco Goya."

Me thinking: "Wow, that is cool."

Sitton continuing: "It's also the birthday of my major professor, Howard Thomas!"

Me, still thinking: "Now that's outstanding!"

Sitton's finale: "And March 30th is my birthday! I'm not impressed with your paintings, but it's impossible to ignore your birthday. You are accepted in our MFA program. You'll have to work hard to stay in it, but for now, welcome to Georgia State University."

And that was that. I start classes in September. I'm determined to show that Mr. Jim Sitton that I am an artist worthy of my birthday. He might even like my work one day.

I'll write more soon and may even try to make a road trip down to Mobile to see you. My love to you and your family.

Love,
Margee

Whose Shoes?
Joanne Camp

"Rrrrrip." Lynn had finished writing the first full legal pad page of her answer. I was still studiously reading the scenario and jotting notes. Our law school course had only one exam to determine if you passed. For students used to pop quizzes and mid-term exams before the final test, it was a hard skill to accomplish. All the information that you gathered during the course had to be applied to two or three scenarios that the law professor would propose. The tests were subjective, and grades were based on how much knowledge of the subject you could dump on a legal pad in the time allotted for the test.

I squeezed three years of law school in between two children. My oldest accompanied me on the path to law school acceptance. I took the LSAT, the aptitude entrance exam, with morning sickness, mentally cursing the student next to me who was eating lollipops at 7:30 in the morning. Test results, application, and letters of recommendation were submitted, and I was one of forty-five persons accepted to the Jones School of Law in Montgomery. I was one of four women and the only one with a three-month-old baby at home.

The classrooms were housed in the old chapel on the Huntington College campus, but the school was owned by the University of Alabama. All the students at Jones had day jobs, except for Ann Laura, who was a retired teacher. Most of the students worked with the state government in the legislative or judicial branch. A few had jobs in the private sector such as Don, an insurance salesman, and Lynn, who worked in the securities division of a bank. We all gathered from those jobs at seven in the evening and attended lectures for two hours three days a week, a different course each night. The instructors themselves had day jobs. In my first semester, the clerk of the Court of Civil Appeals taught Legal Research, the city attorney for Montgomery taught Contracts, and two cute young personal injury attorneys taught Torts.

My day job was as a legal secretary to the Lee County Circuit Judge. Although my background was in languages, while I was translating and researching for "No Such Agency" in Washington, D.C., a girlfriend talked me into taking a paralegal course. This, along with the talent of shorthand, a skill I picked during my college years, won me the position. Shorthand also helped me take precise and copious law school notes. I studied each weekend by transcribing the notes into typed manuscripts.

Between work and school and studying, my husband became our son's primary caretaker. As the end of law school was on the horizon, I became pregnant with our second child, strategically timed to be born the week after I finished the term. I was the only pregnant woman in my law school class.

The first test at the end of the first semester, Contracts, eliminated half of the class. Our numbers went from forty-five hopeful students to twenty-two stalwarts. I received the highest grade for that test with a "C," the lowest grade I had ever received in my educational career, except for typing and trampoline. But like survivors of great adversity, the remaining students became a close-knit group. Many nights after class, we would gather at a local pub to commiserate about our lives and occasionally convinced the professor to join us. With my pregnancy, I became the "designated driver" of the carpool that drove Interstate 85 from Auburn to Montgomery those three nights a week.

One of the classes that I took during my last semester was Trial Advocacy. The course was a continuation of the legal research we studied our first semester, applying our learned skills to a realistic legal problem. Analysis of the case and application of the appropriate and winning law was the objective. Instead of a written final exam, our law professor drafted the services of three attorneys, unknown to us, to serve as judges. To add to the gravity of the test, we would perform our arguments in the Holy of Holies of judicial practice, the Alabama Supreme Court building.

To even approach the Supreme Court building, you climbed steps wide as the building itself. Eight granite columns stretched across the front. Once inside eight more marble columns supported the rotunda that seemed to be a footstool for God. The building smelled of furniture polish and old books and commanded silence in the hall.

Jack, my partner in the endeavor, and I had spent hours in research and preparation, honing our arguing points and polishing the written brief. Our adversaries were classmates, Avery and Pat. Both teams strove to be the best. We were the first pair of teams to present our case that evening, and I was the only woman in all four teams.

We organized our paperwork at one of the desks that faced the wood-paneled dais where our three judges would sit. On the center panel of the seating bank was a huge Seal of Alabama. To add to our nervousness, each podium was equipped with a tiny traffic light. Green meant you could argue, yellow that you had two minutes, and red meant stop, even if in mid-sentence. Each of us would have seven minutes to argue our cause.

With nerves and a fetus pressing on my bladder, I knew I needed a bathroom break before we started. I wandered the floor looking for the restroom. I could find a men's room, but no women's room. I drafted Jack, Avery, and Pat to look, also, but with no luck. In my mind, I reasoned, there were no women Supreme Court Justices (at this time), and very few practicing women attorneys. They must only have a men's room, I thought.

"Guard the door," I commanded my three classmates as I walked into the empty restroom. Concealed behind the stall door, with only my black high heel pumps showing, I heard someone else enter. Looking down, I saw a pair of polished wingtip shoes.

"Jack, is that you?"

"The ladies' room is on the third floor," an unfamiliar man's voice responded.

When I left the bathroom, there was no one in the hallway. I returned to the courtroom and joined Jack at the desk. Pat and Avery had their heads down, studying their scripts. Jack was rearranging papers. The three attorneys sat behind the paneled bench, austere and expectant.

"Joanne, you're up," our professor prompted. I walked to the podium. The baby in my belly and my stomach both did somersaults. The green light came on.

"Your honors …" I began, but all I could think was "Whose shoes did I see?"

Chapter 4
Amore or Less

Stalking Mr. Diamond
Gail Smith Langley

The first boy I loved was David Diamond. He appeared out of the ether one autumn morning as I trudged to school. It was actually a beautiful morning draped in a decoupage of tinted autumn leaves. With no appreciation for the stunning southern fall surroundings, I lumbered on carrying a disgruntling load of heavy books. This was my eighth school year of drudgery. In the mid-century, backpacks were only an item in the world of hikers and paratroopers. No rest for the weary student.

Suddenly there appeared a god, David Diamond, overtaking me on the path typically walked by mere mortals trekking their way to the village school.

Before I could gather my senses, the heavens opened and stardust fell, filling my heart with a love so strong that I could not take in a single breath of the rarified Alabama air. Words I would reconsider for years to come escaped my lips. "Sweet Jesus!" I cried in shock as David Diamond lifted the books from my arms. All at once, the golden leaves fell from the trees in a swirl around David Diamond, coloring the wonder of the moment. Birds lost their senses and began to sing in harmonies. It was then a realization overcame me. A boy dreamier than Tab Hunter was now holding my books and talking to me, as if I were worthy. I have no idea of the conversation due to struggling to simply breathe. I fell hard for David Diamond that day.

As night fell, I inserted a lavender ink cartridge into my Scripto pen. I recorded in my most careful script, *Mrs. David Diamond, Mrs. David Diamond, Mrs. David Diamond, Mrs.*

David Diamond, and on and on, using up several precious pages in my vinyl-covered five-year diary. The book-carrying incident was written in mostly accurate details ... maybe not the part about David Diamond kissing my hand. Later entries involving David Diamond were products of a love only imagined while I continued to long for My Special Love.

By October, David Diamond was exclusively carrying Cassie Walton's books. Cassie was the poster girl for who's who in popularity. (I swear she was buck-toothed.) She wore his class ring around her neck. As I explained to my diary, my ardent love was not dampened by his attention to Cassie. I continued stalking David Diamond. All known facts I gathered from secretly following him and several not so accidental meetings. These were carefully recorded each night in my journal. "David Diamond is letting his curly blond hair grow. David Diamond's eyes are sexier than Ricky Nelson's." I would write through the night or at least until nine o'clock when my parents checked for lights out.

Intense scrutiny revealed that David Diamond was from exotic Canada, somewhere north of New York City and Tennessee, where I imagined he bravely struggled against polar bears and icefloes. He proved himself to be brilliant and self assured by standing in a school assembly, before the entire school body, and declaring that communism reminded him of a horrible black bear. Such profound thoughts came easily to David Diamond. I was so proud to be his secret love.

During my senior year, in a fit of maturity, I recovered my senses. I took the same path to school. I was strolling in yet another temperate, glorious autumn day. Truly, I did not have even the smallest conscious thought of David Diamond. I was way too sophisticated for silly schoolgirl crushes. Also, Ben McCreary was carrying my books. I might add, Ben McCreary's eyes are prettier than Ringo Starr's.

The Decision
Joanne Camp

Through the large plate glass window that surrounded Bob's by the Bay, a local bar, I could see the sailboats swaying lazily on Chesapeake Bay. Diamond-white sailboats with sultry teak hardware had their sails cinched neatly to the yardarms. Along the only wall that did not showcase a window was a long bar, the same teak as the sailboats. It L-ed into a short portion that accommodated four stools. Jimmy and I claimed the middle two to be by ourselves. The remainder of the bar was full of couples. It was Valentine's Day 1976. There were a few loners sitting at the bar, but everywhere people were paired.

When it came time to order drinks, Jimmy chose his usual beer. He leaned on the bar, the bottle cupped between his hands. He gazed at me with the clear pool-blue eyes that I could drown in. The light through the window highlighted his blond hair. I thought of the song lyrics, "sprinkled moon dust in your hair of gold and starlight in your eyes of blue."

Pulling myself back, I pondered, "What would a sophisticate order?" The bartender sensed my indecision.

"How about a Pink Lady?" It sounded intriguing and trendy, so I agreed. Shortly a pink frothy-topped beverage in an open champagne glass sat before me. We toasted Jimmy's trip to the D.C. area.

We settled into a comfortable silence and watched the reflections of the sunset on the harbor. Jimmy began fidgeting with a package of matches provided by the bar as an advertisement and courtesy to smokers. Jimmy smoked. I had never. He handed me the matchbook. I took it from him with a quizzical frown. He responded with his soft relaxed smile. In a quiet, close voice, he said, "I want you to keep these so that you remember where I asked you to marry me."

I was stunned and did not answer. A tear slipped from my eye, which caught the bartender's attention.

"You like the drink? Is it okay?" I nodded, afraid if I spoke, I would bawl; afraid if I looked into Jimmy's sky-blue eyes, I would say the wrong thing.

After a few moments of uncomfortable silence, Jimmy slid off his stool.

"I'll be right back," he said and headed toward the restroom sign. Once he was out of sight, my eyes welled, and I bit my lip. I grabbed a napkin and dabbed my eyes.

I had loved Jimmy for the five years we had been dating. When he said that he would fly up to Maryland to spend the weekend, I was thrilled. Though I had been there a year, this was the first time he had ventured close to the Mason-Dixon line to visit me in the D.C. area. When we graduated, I had the opportunity to move away from the little southern town of Opelika to the big city. My Russian professor urged me to interview with the National Security Agency when they came to the Auburn campus for potential employees. Their information sheet indicated that the NSA was looking for electrical engineers and math majors, but my professor, a former NSA employee, encouraged me to apply.

Within a few weeks, I received a job offer, pending my background check. Friends and acquaintances began receiving visits from the local FBI, including Mr. Dubose, who ran the small station from which I occasionally bought gas on credit.

His response to the federal agent's question about whether I drank was, "Of course, she's Catholic, ain't she?"

I was on my way to living my fantasy life — using my languages, Russian and Spanish, in the big city, and as a bonus, I was a spy. I kissed my big Catholic family goodbye, packed my Chevrolet Vega with everything I owned, and drove seven-hundred and fifty miles to Alexandria, Virginia, to stay with a friend while I searched for an apartment.

A month later, I had my own apartment just outside the beltway of Washington, D.C.; a security clearance with a matching badge; and a salary larger than any of my friends who had graduated from the foreign language department. I reveled in city life, taking the subway into "the City" each weekend to visit the Smithsonian or the National Museum. Some Sundays I would drive my car around until I was totally lost and with maps and landmarks find my way back to my apartment. I went home to Opelika only for Christmas. My fellow workers and I spent most Friday nights at chic bars in Columbia or Baltimore. I was entrenched in the area and determined that I would make my mark here on my terms.

I took classes at the University of Maryland and got a paralegal certificate because a supervisor hinted that it would be a quick way of getting a promotion. I was on the short list of linguists to begin a five-year Russian studies program that would move me to the coveted seventh floor where the "Tom Clancy" analysts worked.

After I left Alabama, Jimmy and I kept in touch with long letters declaring our devotion and mooning over the distance that separated us. But I did not offer to return to Alabama, and he resisted moving to "the North." He had lived in Opelika since he was three; it was his home. Although he was stability, personal and financial, I needed to become my own person and never wanted to live in small-town Alabama again.

I had driven as far south as North Carolina to meet him, and once in a fit of foolishness and desire, I had ridden an Amtrak train for twenty-four hours for our rendezvous in Boca Raton, Florida. We were in love, but I had chosen career over commitment.

When Jimmy returned to the bar stool, I said that we needed to leave for the restaurant, as we had reservations for the evening at one of the famous Chesapeake Bay restaurants. Their specialty was a steamed basket of crab, clams, and bay delicacies. Hand in hand, we walked, in a comfortable, harmonized step, a few blocks through Annapolis to a packed restaurant. We were directed to the bar, which served as a waiting room for patrons hopeful of obtaining a table. I sat on the only available stool, while he stood in front of me, caressed my hand, and softly encouraged me to give him an affirmative answer. We crooned words of love. But not receiving a commitment, he went to check on our reservations. I began to sniff again and stared at my hands in my lap. Gentle fingers touched me on the shoulder. Next to me sat two nuns in floor-length black habits and veils with their backs to the bar also awaiting their table.

The closest asked, "Is there anything wrong?"

Her soothing voice broke the last barrier maintaining my composure, and I blubbered, "My boyfriend just asked me to marry him, and I don't know what to do."

They both looked in Jimmy's direction, standing in front of the maître d', a handsome, suited man taking care of arrangements.

They looked at each other with beatific smiles and turned to me.

"Marry him, dear, he looks like a nice man."

When he returned, I was calm; I had made up my mind. The two nuns were smiling at him. He nodded at them politely. He extended his hand to me. I took it, hopped off the stool, and we followed a waiter to our table. We ordered another drink. This time, I settled on a beer. While we were waiting for our order, I reached across the table and squeezed his hand with both of mine.

"Yes, I said, "I'll marry you. But I never want to live in Opelika again."

He squeezed my hands and agreed. "Of course, of course."*

*Since that time, we have lived in Opelika and Auburn.

Ted Nixon, Where Are You?
Katie Lamar Jackson

Ted Nixon where are you? At the KOA campground on Apollo Road? At some Lafayette club gliding around the dance floor to the music of the Branch Playboys? Back in Michigan selling used cars? In heaven with Grace?

I wish I knew because, just now, I'd sure like to dance with you.

You may not remember me but one night many years ago you asked me for a dance in Breaux Bridge, Louisiana. I was there to see the Evangeline Oak and to prepare myself for what I knew was the impending end of a long-term romance. I was feeling blue and didn't want to spend the evening holed up in my room at a no-name motel in St. Martinsville, so I took myself out to dinner at the nearby and world-famous Mulate's cajun restaurant.

As I sat there all alone eating gumbo, drinking Blackened Vodoo beer, and listening to the house band, the numbing sorrow I'd been feeling about my romantic situation began to ease. When a large group of hefty Germans, all draped in Mardi Gras beads (despite the fact that Fat Tuesday had come and gone months before) began to polka around Mulate's wooden dance floor to the band's zydeco tunes, I found myself smiling. And when the Germans asked the waitress to "talk Cajun" to them and she kept saying "I ain't a Cajun," I laughed out loud. My toe also started tapping to the music, but being without a partner or much natural grace, I stayed rooted to my chair. That is until you approached and asked me to dance.

"I don't know how," I said.

"I'll teach you," you replied, and before I could protest, you led me to a back a corner of the restaurant and instructed me on a basic waltz and a little two-step before leading me onto the dance floor to try out my new-found moves. You kept telling me to relax — to let go and just follow you — and soon we were skimming across the boards, weaving our way through the stomping Germans. You made it easy. And you were right. Once I followed your lead, I could also follow my instincts.

Between sets, we sat at a small table and you told me that you and Grace, your wife of many years, had begun attending Cajun dances in Detroit, which struck me as an odd place to find Louisiana music, but who was I to question it. I learned that your love of dancing had led you to vacation in and around Lafayette, Louisiana, parking your motor home at the KOA campground and going out nightly to hit the many dance clubs in the parish. I learned that the two of you had big plans to spend winters at that campground once you retired. Then I learned that, just as you were retiring, Grace got sick. She was gone in a matter of months.

"I decided I should come to Lafayette anyway," you said. That's when you told me about a Catholic priest who had lived on Cape Breton in Canada's Acadian region. Unlike his predecessor who had frowned on frivolity and discouraged fun, this priest encouraged his parishioners to enjoy life and especially to play music and move their feet.

"When you dance, you trample the troubles of the world," the priest had reportedly said.

"I'm taking his advice," you said. "I'm here to dance and trample my troubles."

After that story, I was totally smitten by you, so when you asked if I wanted to follow you around on a zydeco dance bar crawl, I didn't hesitate to say "yes." I trailed behind the taillights of your red convertible, which sported a vanity tag reading "Yahoo," to every music joint we could find in Lafayette Parish. We danced around and across their dance floors until almost dawn before saying goodbye in a gravel parking lot where we exchanged only a hug — no phone numbers; no addresses — before going our separate ways.

Not long after I returned home, the romance ended, and despite being prepared for that inevitability, it still hurt. But it hurt less because of you, Ted. And today, more than three decades later, our single evening together continues to help me waltz through life.

I wish I could tell you that now, but I don't know where to find you so this will have to suffice.

Thank you, Ted Nixon, wherever you are. And yahoo!

Chapter 5
The Royal Issue and Other Children

Fortress
Mary Dansak

I built my house with wildflowers and wine,
with tumbling critters, and scoundrels and tramps
and extra dogs, and movie nights,
so when they came for me
with Sunday School pitchforks and PTA bombs
and endless pleas for brownies, more brownies!
I gathered my husband and daughters together
in jangled, tangled arms and replied,
"But we don't have an oven."

Low Christmas, High Christmas
Gail Smith Langley

The only son and only child, Rivers Andrew, at some point, realized that Santa Claus was a ruse. He came to this awakening later than his friends and classmates, or at least he refused to let go of the notion that a mystical elf brought so much largesse down chimneys. (After all, the cookies and milk left by the fireplace certainly disappeared.) As a test for Santa's authenticity, the kid hid his Christmas wish list between the sofa's velvet cushions. "If you are real, Santa, you will find this message. I've been a good boy, and here's my list." Luckily by happenstance, St. Nicks' big helper found the note, left some crumbs on the cookie plate, and fulfilled some of the boy's lengthy list.

As all these stories go eventually with reason, or more likely due to classmate ridicule, Santa was put away with other childish things. For a while, the boy's faith in his parents had slipped more than his faith in Olde St. Nick.

How to appease the loss and make the future elfless holiday jolly? We were a small family with no nearby relatives to enhance happy holiday gatherings or to fill the loss of St. Nick. Only the three of us were left to bolster the season's cheer. The first year after notions of an imaginary sky sleigh rider had been dismissed, we vacationed in Orlando's Disneyworld. There Mickey, Minnie, Donald, Daisy, and Pluto were family enough for us. Our decorated Tannenbaums dimmed in comparison with Cinderella's Castle. Santa's helpers were easily replaced with Chewbacca, Darth Vader, and Teenage Mutant Ninja Turtles.

In snowless Alabama, we could only imagine a sleigh ride in a wintry wonderland. Still, the one-horse open sled could not be as much fun as Splash Mountain. Not as heart-racing as Space Mountain. Certainly not possibly as entertaining as Buzz Lightyear's Space Ranger Spin.

This Disney vacation was the beginning of our "Low Christmas" traditions. We altered the holidays by celebrating High Christmas at home and Low Christmas by traveling. Over the years, we snorkeled in the Florida Keys. We shivered in the Smoky Mountains. Occasionally some foreign travel was thrown in. We happily replaced presents with journeys.

When it was time for "High Christmas," the three of us stayed home, delighting in all the traditional yuletide celebrations; tree, stockings, lights, turkey, eggnog, and best of all, presents, after not having any the year before. Because High Christmas occurred only every other year, I would give considerable and lengthy thought to the unique gifts to put under the tree.

Eventually, the two kinds of celebrations dissolved. The grown son flew the coop and became only a seasonal visitor. Because he was so rarely at home, we gave up Low Christmas and traveling to enjoy time together. We settled into High Christmas mode.

In anticipation for the Yuletide, I found myself scrambling to organize a spectacular 2019 holiday. I was in need of inspiration for amazing presents. I wanted to buy Husband Bob an iPad. Unfortunately, the husband is an analog kind of guy who, in his luddite status, proudly resisted change in a world gone digital. Begrudgingly he accepted moving to an iPhone after his dinosaur phone went kaput. Since having taken a few

The Mystic Memoir

technological baby steps, I thought he would love an iPad after the initial high-tech shock of receiving it wore off. Well, maybe not love it, but tolerate the intrusion of the modern world. As an inducement, not to return the iPad to the store, Rivers Andrew had downloaded his dad's favorite music. With a touch of the finger, Bob would be in Stevie Nicks' heaven. To clinch the deal, a few fishing apps were added along with The Weather Channel. What could go wrong?

Finding an appropriate and desired present for a grown kid was sincerely difficult. I admit, after tossing around possibilities, I gave in and requested a gift list. The appeal produced the usual response, "money." Still, I wanted something a bit more imaginative than currency. Something unique that spoke to the recipient.

The inspiration materialized from a random comment by a friend of Rivers Andrew's. We have a collection of countless childhood photographs that validates his comic nature. A perfect example was his sixth-grade school picture. He was wearing his Cirque du Soleil hat, which was a screaming orange beanie topped with a duster of lime feathers. This is actually a milder selection of the kid's Kodak moments. Such pictures occasionally made their way to social network postings. Because, the photographs were truly hilarious, his friend commented, "I'd like to have a goofy Rivers Andrew calendar."

Eureka! The special gift solution began to take shape. In the coming days, I scoured the numerous childhood scrapbooks, shuffling and reshuffling the funniest. Finally, after hours of choices and cuts, I had the perfect twelve.

A local printing company exceeded my expectations, and the final calendar made me laugh out loud. It was a pure joy. It was perfect. At great expense, I had fourteen calendars printed, two copies for me, the adoring mother, and twelve for Rivers Andrew to keep and distribute to friends. I could hardly wait till Christmas morning as anxious as any child waiting to unwrap presents.

Rivers Andrew slept late. Then breakfast, and finally it was time to open the gifts, starting with the most special calendar. After a quick unwrap the child, now man, exclaimed, "Oh my God, I hope no one has seen this. You better not give this to a living soul! I'm warning you, Mom. This is horrible. What were you thinking?"

I was devastated. So downcast, in fact, that I was in a fog remembering little of the other presents. I do remember that Bob, upon unwrapping his iPad, exclaimed how much he loved it and how he had been hoping for just that. We looked at him in Christmas amazement. In this rare, improbable moment, the spirit of Santa appeared unexpectedly to the non-believers.

A Brief on Child Rearing
Joanne Camp

Good Mother vs. Good Student

I turned the thermometer slightly up and then down until the glint of mercury glowed. One hundred four degrees. Still one hundred four degrees.

My tow-headed toddler's warm head lay on one of my thighs; my legal research text lay on the other. I leaned over and pressed my lips to his sweaty forehead. My momma's thermometer told me the instrument was correct. I had given him the prescribed dose of baby Tylenol over an hour ago. The bottle advised that I could not give him another for three more hours. I swapped my law book for the childcare book and researched fever. "If a child's fever does not reduce with medication, give him a lukewarm sponge bath."

It was Sunday night. No pediatrician or doctor's office was open. I would not expose him to the chaos of the local emergency room. My husband had left for a business trip early in the afternoon, flying to Maine. Our only child had been active when he kissed his daddy goodbye and stood on the front step waving until his daddy's car turned the corner. By dinnertime, my son refused to eat his macaroni and cheese and by seven o'clock, he was listless and warm.

I prepared the bath, lukewarm water only four inches deep in the porcelain tub. Then rousing him, I sat him in it and sponged the water over his back and chest. Bath time was usually playtime for him, but he sat slumped like a defeated warrior. Wrapped in a thick blue towel, he nestled next to me on the couch again. I took his temperature. It was slightly lower. I checked my watch to see how soon I could administer Tylenol.

With one hand, I alternated touching his forehead and back checking for a rise in fever. With the other, I followed the words in *Plessy v. Ferguson* and *Brown v. the Board of Education*. I had a dozen cases to prepare for tomorrow's law school class. My son stirred and whimpered, and I placed a marker on the page, and pulled him over into my lap. I rocked him and sang his favorite lullaby "Sweet Baby James" until he quieted. The night continued, another dose of Tylenol, another few pages read, another lukewarm bath.

Finally, well past both our bedtimes his fever broke, I finished my reading and notes, and we both fell exhausted into bed. Our Monday morning routine took my son to my mother's home and me to my job. After work I drove my carpool to law school. I settled into my desk with assurance that I had briefed all the cases and was ready for any Socratic query. As the rustle of papers and shuffling of books settled, the professor entered and began writing on the blackboard. I opened my textbook and the pages parted to the last case I read. There, marking the spot, was a baby thermometer.

Docket Call

"You mean your daddy is an attorney, and your mommy goes to work." My son's teacher was asking each second-grade student what their parents did during the day.

"No," Jeremy's answer started low and went up two notes, as if he were explaining the matter to a seven-year-old, rather than being the seven-year-old. "My mommy is an attorney, and my daddy goes to work."

My two sons knew what their mommy did for a living because they sometimes accompanied me to the office. School holidays, which were not court holidays, or some days during summer break, would find them coloring in my conference room. They knew that their daddy got up early each morning, put on a suit and went to work. Where was a mystery to them.

One Monday morning, I arrived at the office with my eight-year-old and five-year-old with me. My secretary greeted me with a reminder of a nine o'clock docket call with my two files neatly arranged under the notice, and the additional reminder that she had an eight-thirty dentist's appointment.

In the interest of judicial economy, judges will set a docket, a listing of pending cases, to determine status and to rule on pending motions. While the parties involved in the case are not usually required to come, all attorneys representing those parties must attend. Although they are open to the public, docket calls rarely attract onlookers or reporters.

Gathering the files, a pen, a legal pad, two coloring books and a box of crayons, I herded my sons into the car and to the courthouse. The courtroom has a press box, a separate room at the back from which the members of the fourth estate can witness a trial through a wall of windows. Sounds of the trial are transmitted through anyone speaking into a microphone in the courtroom from either the judge's bench or the witness stand or the microphones located at two attorney's desks in the courtroom area. Private conversations between a client and his attorney, or bench conferences cannot be heard. Inside the room, under the window is a long counter, with chairs tucked underneath so reporters can take notes during trials or use computers.

I placed my young sons in the press box, with the coloring books and crayons, and a threat that they would never see another Teenage Mutant Ninja Turtles program again if they did not behave. I then walked into the courtroom to join the several attorneys gathered for the same docket. I could see my children; they could see me. I hoped none of my other colleagues, or the judge, would notice.

The docket call dragged on in its tedium. Some company vs. somebody. Some creditor vs. some debtor. And so on. I watched the clock tick by, too aware of the attention span of a five-year old and an eight-year-old boy. An hour and a half later, the last case was called, and business completed. Everyone rose as the judge left his post.

The court reporter had been taking down all the proceedings. He had been helpful in my legal training. After my trials he would discuss aspects of my case that I could have done better, or parts of the opponent's case that were weak. And he loved children. As soon as the judge left, he walked over to one of the attorney's benches, and announced through the microphone, "Boys, are you hungry?" My sons looked at me expectantly through the window. When I nodded consent, they scampered out of the press box and into the courtroom. The court reporter took each boy in each hand and announced, "We'll be back in a minute."

As I gathered my paperwork, and the crayons and coloring books, the boys returned with a candy bar in one hand and a soda in the other.

In Re: The Matter of Juvenile Court

Twelve years into my law career, as my oldest was completing high school and my younger starting high school, I was blessed with another blue bundle of joy. Like his older brothers, he was sometimes an assistant in my law-doings. The clerks, judges, and other officials were used to his presence on those necessary occasions.

My practice gravitated to juvenile law, representing children in criminal matters, or when they did not want to go to school, or when they had incompetent parents, or when they refused to obey competent parents. These proceedings were closed to the public, and in actual hearings, my youngest would not be present.

However, like docket calls, the judge would call out all pending cases to find out the status so as not to leave any child behind. Judge called down the list, and while none of the children were in the courtroom, their other attorneys answered "here" for them.

I should have seen the gleam in Judge's eye, but I was busy with my files and paperwork, my son sitting quietly behind me. At the bottom of the list, Judge added, "Jake Camp." I looked up startled, but my son stood to his four-foot height, and promptly answered, "Here, your Honor."

The Year of the Horse
Katie Lamar Jackson

The moment I saw the small golden horse statue on our table at a 2014 Chinese New Year dinner party, a decoration proclaiming the incoming Year of the Horse, it was all I wanted from the evening and the year. So, yes, I rustled that gilded pony and brought it home with me thinking it would make a fine present for one of my offspring or for one of their offsprings.

Why? Because I believe there is no finer gift for children than a pony, a fact I know from personal experience.

I was born into a horse-infatuated family. (It may truly be genetic.) Both of my parents were equestrians, and according to family legend, my mother was riding horses throughout her pregnancy with me, so perhaps this passion was engrained in me before I even arrived into the world.

Whatever the reason, I always, ALWAYS, wanted a horse of my own, and by the time I was eight years old, owning my own horse was an obsession. We already had a big bay named Rap who was, in theory, the family's horse, but he was too big for me to ride alone. I needed something smaller. I needed a pony, and I decided the best way to acquire said pony was from Santa. So that year I devised a plan: "a pony" was the only item on my Christmas list, a tactic I felt sure would leave Mr. Claus no choice but to deliver on my sole demand.

That Christmas morning, however, no pony stood in the living room next to the stockings nor was one tethered outside the back door. There were other gifts for me, which was troubling because their presence suggested Santa had ignored my request.

Later that morning, as I followed our parents to the barn to feed Rap, my small heart was broken. That is until I experienced my own Christmas miracle in the stable. A fat black pony stood in a stall, fetlock deep in yellow straw with red ribbons woven into its mane and tail. I clutched my hands to my chest and, according to my mother, breathlessly gasped, "There is a Santa Claus!"

That miraculous creature, whose name was Matizable, was not mine alone. I had to share her with my two siblings, but I knew she would not have appeared had I not wished her into existence. So, in my young mind, she was MINE.

Matizable turned out to be not only stunningly black, but also stunningly possessed by black magic. She was as unmanageable as she was beautiful, probably through no fault of her own; she'd likely had enough experience with other young riders to know her best defense was a good offense. She threw us off, balked at any command to move forward, and often nipped and squealed at us. I tried to win her love with bribes of carrots, apples, and sugar cubes, but she never warmed to me, and after a few months' trial, our parents decided she should be returned to Santa Land.

Though heartsick at the loss of my Christmas miracle, by then I was also afraid enough of Matizable that I did not protest too loudly. Thankfully my parents soon procured another black pony named Mary who was as sweet as she was patient. That dear creature was part of our family for another three decades, living to the ripe old age of forty, long enough to carry my own children around on her barrel back.

Mary was also one in a long parade of horses that came into my young life, including the first horse that I could truly call my own. Thanks to a $500 loan from my grandfather on my fifteenth birthday, I purchased a green-broke chestnut quarter horse-thoroughbred gelding with a wide white blaze. I named him Little Brother because he was as stubborn as my own little brother, and he was not a perfect horse, but he was mine, all mine.

Over the next few years, Little Brother was the center of my world. I spent hours training, feeding, and grooming him, activities that kept me out of all kinds of teenage trouble and often helped heal my various teenage heartbreaks. And Little Brother remained a constant in my life until, at the tender, foolish age of twenty, I married a man who didn't care for horses.

As newlywed college students, my new husband and I couldn't afford to keep Little Brother, so it only made sense to sell him. And I found the perfect buyer, a lovely woman also named Katie, who I felt sure would love him as much as I did. Still, the day she trailered him away was excruciating. As I stood outside the same stall that had once contained Matizable, I clasped my hands to my chest. I could not breath. I could only sob as my then-husband said, "Why would you cry like that over a horse?" In that moment, I began to realize I may have married the wrong man.

Since then, I've never had another horse that was mine-all-mine, nor have I ever stopped longing for one, and I will always wish I'd been able to give my own children the gift of a horse to love. They're grown now and that opportunity is lost, though these grandchildren ... Wouldn't they love a real pony under their tree? Wouldn't I love to be the one to give them that kind of Christmas memory?

I'll resist for now, but their parents should be forewarned, the Year of the Horse returns in 2026.

Perfectly Composed
Mary Dansak

My arms reach up high around my husband's neck; his head leans down to mine. His eyes are closed. Perhaps mine are too, but you can't tell with my back to the camera. We're dancing in the living room to "The Wind Cries Mary," Jimi Hendrix of course.

Nothing special happened that night. We were just listening to music, drinking wine, and then dancing. I probably would've forgotten it all together if not for the snapshot.

I'm guessing the photograph was taken in 2001. We'd been married for fourteen years, were living in the second of two states we'd live in, and were parents to three daughters ranging from six to thirteen years old. My brother had recently died unexpectedly, and we'd moved into a new house, two giant shifts in a tumultuous decade.

I was teaching middle school at the time, a relentless vacuum which consumed all my flame. Joe, too, was all-consumed building his massage therapy business. The girls' lives were full of social whirls and music lessons. One year, between violin lessons, piano lessons, Girl Scouts, chorus, and band, there were twenty-seven public appearances for the girls during the Christmas season alone.

We were in survival mode. I was doing well to get canned fruit and tuna fish on saltine crackers onto the girls' plates for dinner. Every Thursday, Joe had a client who paid in cash, which we spent on a Brand X pizza and a bagged salad. I lived for Thursday nights.

Chaos ruled, romance fizzled. When I look back through my photo albums of those days, I am exhausted by the pace laid out in the neatly labeled images, forever enshrined under plastic sleeves.

That picture of Joe and me dancing never made it to an album. It has been roaming around the house ever since it showed up. Currently, it is on display in the kitchen, tacked on a bulletin board along with a smattering of pictures of friends' kids when they were wee and a postcard of Malcom X.

"Look at that picture," Anna, all grown-up, said one day. "I took it with your camera." She reached up and touched the sweet photo. Odd. I had never considered who had taken it. I never questioned how it came to be in that soft white envelope I picked up from CVS.

Anna was studying environmental design at our local university at the time. Her eye for beauty, evident even at six years old, was growing wings.

"Amazing," she said, handing the picture to me. "It's perfectly composed."

I looked at it with new eyes. So it is, I thought, perfectly composed. And somehow, for that one moment now frozen in time, a young couple dancing unawares, so were we

The Hands that Raised You
Katie Lamar Jackson

My Dearest Children,

One of these days, after I'm gone, you will no doubt have questions about your upbringing, which is why I am writing this letter.

As you know, I was never a particularly discipline-inclined parent, though I was borderline ferocious about making sure you were polite to other people and respectful of their feelings, boundaries, and property. Other than that, my child-rearing style was, yes, lenient.

I was more inclined to explain the many reasons I wanted you to do something rather than quip "because I said so," and I usually warned you several times before taking any sort of disciplinary action. When you were very young, I cajoled or sometimes bribed you to do things my way; timeouts were also useful. And it was rare for me to so much as threaten you with a spanking, much less follow through with one. In fact, I can count on one hand the number of times I swatted any of the three of you. I also like to believe those swats only happened when some imminent danger, such as a hot stove or a crumbling cliffside, warranted immediate corrective action. You may recall differently.

Still, you will all probably agree that, when fully provoked, I am renowned for my special version of "lifting a hand" to you, a version that entailed the following very precise steps: with one hand on my hip and my eyes narrowed into slits, I'd raise my other hand and point my index finger in your direction, waggling it while giving you a piece of my mind.

In those moments, which occurred most frequently during your teen years, there was no doubt that you were in trouble. Really big trouble. You had awakened the mythic Kraken in me. Lucky for you, my inner Kraken was usually easy to appease, and I always felt guilty for losing my temper. Well, almost always. Soon I would be back to my old self, as if nothing had ever happened, which was not exactly a model of parental consistency.

I blame, or credit, depending on how you look at it, my waffling ways and my lack of a corporal punishment gene on my parents, who also did not believe in spanking or any form of bodily reprimand. I can only recall two times my mother ever physically chastised me: once when she was upset because I accidentally let Linus, her beloved old Dachshund, outside when he was recovering from back surgery. For that infraction, she popped me on the arm (rather hard in my memory) to show me how easily his healing back could be reinjured if one of our other dogs bopped him with a paw. The other time was when she surreptitiously dug her nails into my arm to make me hush as I chirped out an invitation to a friend to come over and spend the night. Apparently, Mom did not want company that night. Mom also had naturally long fingernails.

My father also spanked me once, two very light taps, but only after he warned me repeatedly that I would be spanked if I didn't stop doing something. What that "something" was is a long-lost memory, yet the dread of that impending spanking, which was more painful than the actual paddling, is still a vivid memory.

It's interesting, though, that despite living in a pacifists' enclave, many of my friends thought I lived in a very discipline-based home because my father was in the military. As a full-time member of the Alabama National Guard, he wore a uniform to work every day. If he showed up for school events or picked me up at a friend's house after work, he was aways in his Army greens, which led many to presume he ran our house like a boot camp, complete with "Reveille" to roust us out of bed.

Nothing could have been further from the truth. As you three know, your grandfather was not the least "hawkish" in his lifestyle or his politics. In fact, the only gun he owned was an ancient hunting rifle that he stowed in a closet after he and Mom married; she did not approve of hunting.

So, as you can see, I came by my lack of parental disciple skills honestly, and while I am sure there were many times when I should have been a more discipline-focused parent, I think all of you turned out quite nicely.

Spare the rod, spoil the child? I think not. But there's a lot to be said for a well-pointed finger.

Love,
Your Imperfect but Peace-loving Mother

Chapter 6
In Your Prime Numbers and Middle Age Crisis

Cruising with the Buckeyes: Who's Minding Ohio?
Gail Smith Langley

This is not my attempt to put down the cruise nation. It's just a truthful account of my misguided spring vacation on The Majesty of the Seas.

So okay. I'm not a cruise person. First of all, the food accurately described as plentiful, I found to be Shoneyesque. My fellow passengers were scrambling to the fare as if this might be their last meals. The frenzy in the self-serve cafeteria resembled the dance employed by bees giving directions to the nearest nectar source.

At night, we dressed for dinner and were served by very polite automatons. In fact, all staffers were curiously kind-mannered, and our personal attendant-valet was almost creep-lurking about the door to our cabin and being obsequious. Whenever we returned to our cabin our person had left napkins folded on the undersized beds in the shape of rabbits and other curious animals.

Other than a handful of a few lost souls, the fellow cruisers were Ohioans. I have nothing against Ohio or its population. I know very little about Ohio. I understand it is a directional state (Midwestern) which seems to me should be located in the middle of Texas, definitely the west, just above Austin. Also, Ohio is the seventh most populated state, a fact which I am fully aware, as I shared a boat with these people. Did the ship offer a Buckeye discount?

I'm wondering, as I write this, if all the Ohioan readers are thinking, "She has some nerve taking about our beloved state. Well, damnnation! She's from Alabama!" Actually, I am fairly entertained by telling people I'm from Alabama. They look at me as if I arrived via a Steven King novel with the ability to kidnap and separate them from their homeland to steal away forever through the Middle Passage.

But this is not about me, so back to the Buckeyes; yes Buckeyes. They are not marked with the sins of their fathers, as are the Heart of Dixieans. Frankly however, I wouldn't want to be saddled with that "Dixiean" moniker either. (Side note, I'm thinking this might be a good time to change our state's nickname.)

I digress, so back to the ship. In musing preparation for the cruise, I imagined that, while strolling the breezy deck, I would pass blanketed readers of varying degrees of chic. They would be enjoying significant essays or creative fiction. We would trade book titles and speak of august ideas. In cruise reality, not one person, not one Ohioan, was reading. Now at my family summers at the Redneck Riviera on the beautiful Alabama coast, where not only do vacationers walk upright, but there are beach readers, pool readers, and patio readers cut from a population of supposed yahoos with a wheel in the ditch.

Making the best of my cruise incarceration, I decided to get some exercise, since I was obviously not going to wax poetic about my latest book find. The ship's customer relations staff frowned at my inquiry when I asked for the time of morning lap swim. They stared at me as if I was an escaped personality disorder. "We don't do morning here," one said in an are-you-out-of-your-simple-mind tone. Wait, what happened to overly polite? "Pool opens at ten this morning," he continued in his irksome pitch.

Not early morning, but the dot of 10:00 am, I loaded up my swim-lap gear and headed to the pool. Goggles, nose clip, ear plugs, fins, tank suit. To my surprise, the entire population of Ohio had already arrived at the pool early and was now occupying the football field-sized pool rim ... lounger-to-lounger. Not an inch between the bathers. They looked exactly like the banana display at Kroger with varying degree of spoilage and spots. The pool itself was teeming with ignored offspring.

Disappointed, I returned my gear to the diminutive cabin where I found an unsettling napkin tortoise on my bunk. Still looking for a bit of exercise, I left for a stroll on the deck. Also out for their morning constitution walk were fifteen or so Buckeyes moving counterclockwise. Maybe that's the human condition. I don't know, but I walked the other way just for the curiousness of watching these people. I passed a group of three young women, possibly mothers who had escaped Akron and carpooling for a girls' holiday. The women were animated talkers and ambulators enjoying themselves immensely. For a second time, I walked briskly by the moms when one snidely commented, "We've lapped that woman twice now."

"You total moron," I thought. "I'm walking the other way!" The fight or flight neurons were jumping around in my brain, as the trio turned onto the stern. I dashed through the ship's glass doors, and across the interior, at super senior speed bursting through the opposite doors, just as the girls turned to walk the port side. I literally passed them just seconds later after I'd seen them. So enlivened in conversation, they didn't seem to notice me, so back through the glass I dashed, just breaking through the door as they finished the bow to walk the starboard side. While they approached, I tried to calm my heart rate and speak casually through my collapsing lungs, "Oh hello!" I panted, "I believe I've lapped you twice this beautiful morning."

Totally unaware of my antics, the sassy one said in protest, "I had to tie my shoe!" At that, the trio turned back to their lively conversation.

I didn't mop my brow until I reached my very tiny, tiny cabin where I took a much-deserved rest with a Bengay rub and a good book, and a creatively folded maybe armadillo.

A Sister's Guide to Grief
Mary Dansak

There is a right way to grieve. That is to carry your solemn soul tucked deep inside, to smile when smiling is called for, to keep the tears unspilled until you are alone when you can thrash and flail and scream.

The right way to grieve is to sort through it, to write your feelings in your journal and work through the stages. What are they? Anger? Denial? Substance abuse? Running naked down the crowded city streets? Burying yourself in your garden with the moonflowers? Sleeping outside in the yard by yourself?

The right way to grieve is to first eat yourself sick on marshmallows and lasagna, bowls of Hershey's kisses, and of course Reese's miniature peanut butter cups, and then to be suddenly averse to food and stop eating all together until one of your friends grabs you by the bony shoulder and gives you a squeeze and says, "Enough." That's the right way to do it.

The right way to grieve is to go to work and look out at your students and wonder why some of them didn't die instead of your brother. A thought like that might condemn you to hell for all eternity, but it's still the right thing to do because, after all, they can't read your thoughts.

The right way to grieve is to put on a big fat hairy act like you know what you are doing as you muddle in the river Styx with the soul of your brother, crawling through the murky waters like a paralyzed soldier, calling his name, reaching, reaching, screaming, "Where are you?" into the dark abyss of death.

The right way to grieve is to go outside in the thunderstorm and sit under a tree, waiting to be struck by lightning because then, then you can find him even though you know he is swirling around you at this moment and in all the moments. His molecules, his energy, his storms are flying now through the night.

The right way to grieve is to laugh in the face of your plans for your tidy life.

It is to crawl on your hands and knees to your stairwell and curl into a fetal position on the third step while your house fills with well-wishers who empty your dishwasher and take your children out to see a new pony and your husband hovers just exactly the right distance away from you, warily and stoically and wisely and tenderly, just right there if you need him but not in your face. You can stay on the third stair all day, or go back to bed, or get up and make coffee, or whatever you need to do because the right way to grieve is to do it so selfishly that everyone gets out of your way.

The right way to grieve is to put on your mourning clothes and stay tucked away for a year.

The right way to grieve is to come back to your senses after your year is up and begin functioning again, properly. Stop all this living on the thin edge of time, like you could die at any minute, or lose someone you love in the blink of an eye. The right way to grieve is to move on. Time heals all wounds, don't you know?

But no. The right way to grieve is to ignore that one-year mark and keep putting one foot in front of another. I know this because I did it and now it's twenty years later and my feet have been steadily trodding out this path of life and I am still here.

Everything I did in the rawness of new death was right. And everything about losing my only sibling, my broken brother, was wrong.

To myself, standing barefooted at my brother's funeral watching my four-year-old daughter turn somersaults in the grass, wondering how I will ever move forward again, I offer this old, tired hand. Come along, come along, there is no right and wrong anymore. Just come along. Come along, you're doing it right.

This essay was originally published in *The Forge Literary Magazine*, August 2022.

Inspiration Oaks
Gail Smith Langley

I have visited many a questionable place and traveled some lengthy roads in pursuit of art finds. This search was a repeat. I'd found my way to River Road before ... how many years? Maybe eight, could be ten. With a measure of trepidation, I turned into a canopy of weighted trees and rutted earth road. I was alone as my husband opted to stay behind at the shore, captivated by the calm sea with a possibility of fish. I was feeling isolated, vulnerable, and unnerved yet willing to handle the trepidation for a visit with Florence and perhaps purchase her art, a swampy version of Grandma Moses.

The first time I saw Florence Landry, she was suspended in wait at the end of a sad driveway. No telling how long Florence had taken up sentry, standing like all time in a pair of Keds that had started life white and heels untrodden. Although all of Florence was, in a word, interesting, her costume and particularly the ancient apron, sized for a bigger woman, was an exact twin to my grandmother's calico back-crossing pinafore. Completing the outfit was a pair of owl glasses with one frosted lens. Florence resembled an asylum inmate who had slipped her charges.

I was late. My given directions were otherworldly. "Here you are," she said. "Don't mind me. I look a sight. I've been putting up jars of about everything, tomatoes mostly." She took my hand and continued. "Now don't let me scare you." She pointed to the opaque glass, and continued, "I ain't got a right eye. But the left is good. Most times I forget to even put on my company glasses."

I navigated from the memories of that first encounter. As I moved through the mottled shadows cast by the detritus of gnarled trees and dark secrets, I lost my confidence in finding my way by recall. I remembered the house, set low against the winds and landmarked by the netted wings of a rough-hewn shrimp boat tethered to a ramshackle dock.

The voice of my GPS suddenly urged me to "RETURN to the Road." And the voice of good sense and reason agreed. So far, there was nothing familiar on my route. Certain I was lost, I looked for a turnaround that didn't seem to be a possibility. Eventually the boggy road arched to follow the river. A house appeared through a miasma of Spanish moss and dark secrets. "The first house past the clearing," Florence had said those years ago.

"This must be it," I thought." Yet, no shrimp boat, and furthermore, no pier stood as landmarks. Chilled by uncertainty, I pulled into an ancient gravel path where rock had coalesced with hard root to form an uncertain driveway. I stopped under suspicious oaks draped in lurking moss.

On the long back porch sat four river folk, still as ramparts, with their eyes on the water and their judgment on me.

I directed the car as close as I dared to the anchored inhabitants. "Hello," I shouted in my best *I come to you in friendship* voice.

Silence. The only reply, a singular cry from an osprey punctuating the gravity of the circumstances.

Finally, as stiff and deliberate as automatons, all four heads turned to solemnly stare at the intruder who had come in peace. Amazingly, their torsos were still facing the channel.

"Is this the Theo Landry place?" I bravely continued. No sound except the river's humming, and perhaps my heart quaking. The air seemed too thin to breathe. The osprey had wisely vanished. "Theo Landry," I repeated.

The nearest grisly soul stood from his seat causing the rocker to metronome perhaps by royal ogre decree. He was a man of sinew and bulk, aged by the sun and hard times. He stared through my soul and muttered just above hearing, one word, "Dead."

The three Gollumesque companions nodded toward the river giving validation to the passing away of Mr. Theo. "Is Miss Florence here?" I weathered on.

His chin lifted up by some invisible marionette string, his eyes piercing through slits. "She don't know you."

"Why yes," I said sweetly. "I've bought her artwork many times."

The giant found his voice, "She don't know herself," he brayed. And with that, a beefy finger pointed at the return of the road. The leviathan lowered himself into the chair having dismissed the interruption and turned toward whatever fascination the river held.

Mumbling again, "Put in the rest home," he said to no one. "She don't know herself."

My car bounded onto Highway 90. I took my first breath in civilization, relieved to find myself escaped. As is my way with all near-death experiences, not that I've suffered many, I began laughing hysterically. So much so, I was a threat to everyone on the road. To gain my equilibrium, I turned into an unlikely placed park. Its sign weathered beyond readable. I knew the words that had lost their paint, Inspiration Oak Park.

Honestly, I had an urge for a cigarette, a habit dismissed years earlier. I opened the car door and walked onto the grounds to get my bearings and composure. The big oak was no longer inspiring, or for that matter, no longer standing. Cut down by a neighbor who disliked the traffic brought to the road by the charm of the enormous tree. I walked to the mammoth stump of inspiration. The park was still handsome, filled by hardwood competitors vying for the downed monolith's fame.

I had managed to calm my hilarity. My mind was on deliverance and on Florence Landry who now didn't know herself. In the beginning our friendship started with a call from a public phone outside an art gallery. This was enough years ago that public telephone booths stood on many street corners. I dialed the number the gallery owner had given me, and Florence answered immediately. Hardly believing my luck, I asked, "Is this Miss Landry?"

"This here is Florence."

"Miss Florence, I'm in town standing outside The Blue Sea Gallery, and have just been admiring your wonderful artwork."

"Yep, those are mine. Which one, honey? The *River Baptism* or *Breezy Clothes Pinned on a Line*?"

"Actually both. I would truly like to meet you, and perhaps purchase some of your paintings."

"Sure honey. I'm home. You can come right on out. Just take 90 to River Road."

"I'm afraid I don't know this area very well."

"Where you're standing is 90. Keep on coming away from town until where they cut down that big tree. Turn left, that's me, River Road. Me and Landry are the first place. Right as you see the river. His shrimp boat is docked there in the backyard. Can't miss that."

I drove miles of Highway 90 until I was fairly certain I'd missed the cut-down tree and the left turn. I pulled into a country store and walked into a time-forgotten place. Somewhere behind the hoop cheese, jars of hard candy, hickory smoked sweet bologna, and eggs floating in vinegar, stood the proprietor.

"Do you by any chance know where the Theo Landry place is?"

"Yessum. You headed to see Florence?"

"I am," relief flooding my voice.

"You are too far this away. He pointed back toward the direction I'd driven. "Go back till you know where they cut down that big tree."

Eventually, I found River Road and the amazing Florence Landry who at that time knew herself.

The Russians Have Come
Joanne Camp

I am in a hotel room in Atlanta, Georgia, with six men; I am the only woman. The room is a suite. A heavy-set man is sitting at a table in the corner. He is dressed in dark casual slacks and a dark long-sleeved button-down shirt. His salt and pepper hair reaches his collar. His eyes are large but sunken and rimmed with dark circles. I attribute them to jet lag.

Sitting at the other side of the round table, his companion is in suit pants with his starched shirt open to the third button. His hair is close-cut and fully dark. He sports a mustache and beard. The other four men are in suits and are standing, their attention turned to these men.

Despite the four-star rating of the hotel, it is furnished in a typical fashion. Two queen size beds butt against the far wall, with pictures depicting landmarks in Atlanta above them. The beds face a chest of drawers upon which sits a television — just like every other room, suite or not. We are in an adjoining space separated by the half wall against which the chest of drawers rests. This adjoining space also has a pull-out sofa, but no one has been invited to sit down.

Perestroika has opened the U.S.S.R. to foreign business. And the seated gentlemen are the First Secretary of the country Georgia S.S.R. and a doctor friend of his. The First Secretary, Patiashvili, is speaking broken English to one of the gentlemen about business contracts in the Russian district. This diplomat from Russia has been invited to the United States to discuss possible interests available between our country and his through a program "Georgians to Georgia." A team of businessmen and politicians from Atlanta and other cities in Georgia are making a similar visit to Tbilisi.

I am the junior partner in a law firm of two in Opelika. My colleague is an established attorney whose thinning carrot top and ruddy complexion, especially when he laughs or is flustered, have earned him the nickname "Red Man." His best friend, Paul, is the client with whom I have driven to Atlanta for this meeting. Paul and Red Man have spent many afternoons after the law office doors are locked enjoying an adult beverage and contemplating ways to become wealthier. Land purchases and business contracts were the usual legal services we did for Paul. As the newest addition to the office, I traveled all over the state, from courthouse to courthouse, investigating titles for potential land developments.

When Paul discovered in one of their late afternoon conferences that I knew the Russian language, his mind went to the possibilities of how that new business territory could benefit him. His research led him to wonder about the harvesting of the virgin forests of Siberia — pulp-wooding in northern Russia. He already had access to the machinery that made such ventures very lucrative in Alabama. Now, he wanted to investigate the possibilities overseas.

It had been over five years since I had used any Russian, and the adage was "If you don't use it, you lose it." So, I checked with some of my previous language professors and found a Russian native, whose husband was a professor at the university, to refresh my knowledge and help me with idioms. We met twice a week in her home for several weeks. In addition to the language, she introduced me to a "day in the life of Russians."

Still with only two years of college Russian, two years of government application of Russian, and a few weeks of review, my speech was elementary, at best. However, armed with that and a Russian-English dictionary, I was prepared to give it my best try.

As the man in the blue suit and red tie finished his presentation, in English, the secretary and his friend nodded but offered no comment. Then, they turned to Paul, but instead, I spoke in Russian, "Здравствуйте, я Джоан Кэмп, адвокат, представляющий моего клиента." ("Hello, I am Joanne Camp, an attorney representing my client.")

I motioned toward Paul. The minister's expression barely changed, but he gestured for me to sit in the only remaining chair. I saw a slight smile on the doctor's face. Paul stood a step closer to me and began firing comments and questions at me to ask the Russians about forests in Siberia. The minister casually answered as he could. It occurred to me that Paul had no idea of where Georgia S.S.R. was nor how vast the Russian country was. But from my limited understanding of pulp wooding, I determined for my client that Siberia had vast crowded stands of virgin timber, especially pines of all types. The problems in harvesting the trees were the short summer season, the long cold winters, and the lack of equipment. I was ready with Russian words for discussions regarding trees, seasons, equipment, and modes of transportation. But then the secretary, prompted by the doctor, mentioned another problem with the harvesting process, БЛОХИ, and КЛЕѡИ, indicating a size with the top of his thumb as he said them. These words sent me scrabbling through my dictionary.

"Fleas and ticks," I reported, "big fleas and ticks during the summer and harvesting season." With that report, Paul frowned and gave the minister his contact information, asking for a forestry connection when the minister returned home.

With that, I thanked the minister and thought my duties were completed. As I stood, another of the waiting people touched me on the shoulder. A young man in his thirties, just slightly older than I was, with clear blue eyes addressed me. His hand lightly remained on my arm as he spoke.

"I'm Thomas. My organization is trying to get Bibles into Russia and to do so, we will agree to send medical supplies along with the Bibles. But I need to know what they would be interested in getting. What medical problems do they have?"

I resumed my seat, and although I directed the question of medical needs to the secretary, the doctor answered. I translated, "They need antibiotics stronger than penicillin."

The gentleman was excited, "We can absolutely do that. What else?"

I spoke directly to the doctor this time. His answer caused me to pause, and blush.

I reported his answer quietly to Thomas so the others would not hear.

"Impotency."

Thomas looked puzzled. "You mean the strength, the potency, of the drugs?"

Reluctantly, I asked the doctor for clarification. He chuckled with his answer, and I blushed again.

"No," I answered, flatly, "impotency — too much vodka."

Capital Murder
Joanne Camp

I cursed under my breath. Or, at least, I thought it was under my breath. When I looked toward the bench, Judge Harper was looking straight at me, eyebrows raised. He was still holding the slip of paper he had just pulled out of a mayonnaise jar sitting on his desk. The jar held the names of all the attorneys in Lee County who had practiced for five years or more. I was the first name drawn to represent a man charged with capital murder. Most of the eligible lawyers were in the courtroom waiting to see if they would win this unlucky lottery. A sympathetic hand patted me on the back. Judge reached into the jar again and announced a second name, "Margaret Brown."

The judge stood. "You ladies and Mr. Myers come see me in my office."

Ron Myers was the district attorney. As the judge left the courtroom, a rumble of relieved chatter rose from the remaining attorneys. I gathered my legal file and purse from the table where I had been sitting; Margaret, who had been standing in the back of the courtroom, finished her conversation with one of the male attorneys. She gave an easy laugh at whatever comment the attorney had made, both were smiling. As we headed to the door, Ron opened it, and with a sweep of his hand in a mock gallant gesture, said "Ladies," as we filed passed him.

In his office, the judge was standing behind the large oak desk seasoned to a gingered brown by age. He was brief and terse, in his usual manner.

"I don't want to try this case twice. I will give you all the time you need to file whatever motions you have to. But let's not try to make this case a career. Ron, you give them what they request. I don't want nitpickin'." With that admonition, he sat and busied himself with paperwork, which was our signal to leave.

"You, girls, get me some discovery motions as soon as you can," the D.A. said as he headed to his office.

"Well, let's go meet our client," Margaret said, and we headed in the opposite direction toward the Sheriff's Department and jail. A long sterile hallway led to the jail. The first stop was a metal door as wide as the hallway. A cabinet high on the wall had four keyed cubby holes for officer's weapons. Next to the door was an intercom panel. Margaret pushed the button, and a familiar voice responded,

"Ma'am? You here to see Jones?"

Margaret smiled, "News travels fast. Yes, Ms. Grigsby, we're here to see Jones."

A buzz let us know that the door was unlocked. I pushed with my shoulder to move the heavy metal. The door slammed solidly behind us as we walked the short distance to the main booking area. Ms. Grisby sat behind a window-paneled room. She was a solidly built black woman, dressed in a tan uniform. She was the first woman to make sergeant in the Sheriff's Department. Having worked there for over twenty years, every one of the deputies, male or female, deferred to her directions when it came to the jail.

"I don't tell Ms. Grigsby how to run her jail, and she don't tell me how to run my office" was the sheriff's answer to anyone who criticized her procedures. She spoke through a microphone.

"How'd you two get so lucky?" she asked with a husky laugh. "Walter's gone to get him. We have him solitary, so it should not be long. You know who he belongs to, don't you?"

"Yeah," Margaret answered, "He's Darrel's nephew."

"Yes, he is, and it's such a shame. Such a nice family." Darrel was one of the probation officers.

I looked through the slotted window of one of the two witness rooms on the opposite side of the area. Margaret motioned for us to go in. Margaret had been practicing a few years longer than I had, but she knew everyone in the system and rarely forgot anyone she had ever met, whether client, witness, juror, or worker at the Justice Center. My practice of law was a general one. I did family law, divorces, wills, and, like most young attorneys, represented my share of indigent criminal defendants during my first years of practice. Margaret's practice was almost exclusively criminal law. I was so glad that she had been appointed to such a serious case with me.

Margaret was a barrel racer and raised and trained her own horses. She did not wear makeup, and her blonde hair grew to her shoulders. Her father had been a cowboy. He was a colorful character who tried to get into a fistfight with a sheriff's deputy who tried to stop him from driving his tractor down the interstate. She had never graduated from high school but began college during her junior year. Consequently, she graduated from law school when she was only twenty-two years old, and immediately began practicing law.

I took a slower route. Going the usual route through high school and college, I worked two jobs before deciding to go to law school. I did not begin practicing until I was thirty years old. I was several inches shorter than Margaret, twenty pounds lighter, and regularly made up my face. We shared the same blonde hair, but I wore mine pulled back or pinned up.

We both sat on the same side of the table, chatting about what we knew of the case when the deputy brought our client. Chris Jones was a tall coffee-colored Black man. He was in his mid-twenties. Even with the jail-issued orange clothing, you could tell that he had been an athlete; he was built like a pro football quarterback. His ankles manacled, he shuffled to the chair opposite us, placed his handcuffed hands in his lap, and waited for us to speak.

Margaret began by introducing us both and letting him know that we had been appointed to represent him, just that morning.

"I've heard of you, Ms. Brown, and Ms. Camp, too," he responded quietly. Margaret continued, explaining generally the charge against him and the seriousness of capital murder.

"Now, I believe if you are found guilty of capital murder, you should be put to death," she began, "but Ms. Camp here is a Catholic, and she doesn't believe that way. So, I'll be trying to have you found not guilty of capital murder, but if you are, Ms. Camp here will get out her beads and try to convince the jury that you should not be put to death. We'll be back to talk to you again as soon as we have all the formal charges against you. Do you have any questions?"

Chris looked at us dumbstruck. Then, he finally answered, "No, ma'am."

As soon as we left the jail, I started into Margaret. "You can't say that! Tell him you believe he should be put to death. He'll never trust us or work with us."

Margaret gave me a grin. "Yeah, I guess I should not have, but he needs to know what we believe."

In the coming weeks, we gathered the indictment and other paperwork regarding the charge. Then we made our discovery request, asking that the state show us what evidence it had against our client. With this information and what our client revealed to us, we tried to put the whole picture together. To the end of obtaining all the evidence the state held, we visited the detective's office after we both had closed our offices down. The investigating officers produced a thirty-three-gallon garbage bag of blood-covered toys and clothes, the couple's child's toys that were present in the room during the massacre, and the clothing that both of them were wearing. Gloved and stoic, we examined every item in the bag. After about an hour, Margaret asked one of the detectives, "Do you think we could have a pizza delivered here?"

The state's case was that our client broke into the victim's house, stole or drank the victim's bourbon, and then stabbed and killed the homeowner when he arrived. Then, our client waited until the man's wife came home, raped her, and tried to kill her, but did not succeed.

Our client's account of the incident stretched credibility. He stated that he was using drugs and went under the couple's house to stay warm. But under the house was a man dressed in Army fatigues who held him at gunpoint and made him do these horrid things. As reasonably as we could, we tried to convince Chris that his story was improbable and that he should trust us and tell us the truth. For many weeks, our encouragement did not convince him to change the story.

Our custom was to visit our client after office hours, an exception permitted by the jail. One day as I waited for Margaret to join me, Chris and I were alone in the interview room. There he began crying and confessed all. I assured him of our pledge of client confidentiality and excused myself to go and check on Margaret. I met her in the hallway and drew her aside.

In a stage whisper, I said, "He told me exactly what happened. He confessed."

Margaret looked at me sternly and replied, "I knew he didn't like me. Why wouldn't he tell me? Nope, he just doesn't like me."

I just shook my head. "Margaret, why does it matter that a capital murderer does not like you?"

On the day of the trial, ours was the only one set. Usually, felonies are set on a trial docket of a dozen or more. The hope is that several will settle, and only one or two cases will be tried, saving the prospective jurors' time. Our case had its special jury venire, the group from which the jury of twelve is chosen, and its own court date. The trial was expected to go on for at least a week, the jury selection alone would take one or two days.

There are two benches, the tables at which the attorneys sit at trial. The district attorney always chose the bench farthest away from the jury box, to face the jury as well as the witness, so he could assess the jurors' reactions to testimony. To the left of district attorney's table was a door leading to a hallway between the two courtrooms, a hall leading only to the other courtroom and the holding cell. From our table, we had a direct view of the witness stand but could only view the jury out of the corner of our eye. To our right was a side hallway that led to the main vestibule.

In the process of jury selection, the attorneys question the people in the pool about their lives and opinions. Based on this information, each side, the state, and then the defense take turns eliminating a person they do not want on the jury until, hopefully, the last remaining twelve are jurors neither side wants, and therefore impartial. Because of the serious nature of our case, there were fourteen jurors at the end of the elimination, the last two serving as alternatives. The alternatives never know their status until the end of the trial. In that way, if anyone were unable to serve through the trial, the entire trial would not have to start over.

Surprisingly, one of the jurors was a friend of my mother-in-law. During the questioning, she admitted that she knew me, so the district attorney called her back for individual questioning. In front of the judge, she put her arm around me, and declared how proud she was that I had "made an attorney." She fussed over me like I was a godchild. But when the district attorney asked if she could listen to the evidence and make an impartial decision, she said that she "reckoned she could" and was left in the group from which we chose. When Ron did not strike her, I asked him why. He smiled and replied, "I'd never strike any of your friends." Infuriating, because he knew this lady would convict her own grandmother.

With the jury seated in their allocated box to the right of our table, my co-counsel and I sat with the accused between us. With everyone in position, the trial began. It was the state's responsibility to build his case block-by-block; it was our task to try to knock one of those blocks down so he would not complete and connect all the points necessary for a conviction. The tedious, but necessary, process went on for three days.

By mid-afternoon of the third day, the district attorney made his closing argument, and Margaret followed. Our strategy was that she would take the lead in the main case. Capital murder cases are bifurcated. The first round is to determine whether the defendant is guilty of capital murder, and the second trial is to determine his sentence — death by the electric chair or life in prison without the possibility of parole. If our client was found guilty of capital murder, then I would take the lead in his sentencing trial because, as Margaret had already shared with our client, I did not believe in the death sentence.

Sitting between us during the entire trial, our client was dressed in a blue suit, white shirt, and navy striped tie. He looked like a college football player ready for a school function. We had given him a pen and legal pad so that he could take notes and jot questions to ask us, but although he kept the pen in his hand, and poised, there was nothing written on the pad.

When the jury filed out to begin its deliberations in a separate, isolated room, the sheriff's deputies led our client to the holding cell located between the courtrooms, and we all began the anxious process of waiting for the jury's decision. The district attorney retired to his office downstairs. Margaret got on her cell phone and began returning calls from the messages that her office forwarded to her.

I paced. One hour. Two hours. The courthouse began to close down at five o'clock. I watched from the second-floor lobby as the parking lot emptied until there were only a few cars left. From that vantage point, I watched the winter sun disappear behind the offices across the street from the Justice Center. About 6:00 p.m., a deputy bailiff called me back to the courtroom. The deputies brought our client in, also, and we sat in the same spots. The D.A. was also there.

"The jury wants to continue deliberating, but I think that I will allow them to go to dinner given the hour," the judge announced. "Any objections?" We surely were not going to object to dinner, although Margaret and I were too nervous to eat or leave the courthouse.

About half an hour later, Margaret came out to get me. "We have got to talk to the Judge," she said, in a nervous tone. "I didn't sign up for this," she added, running her hand through her hair.

"What?" I asked. "What's happened?" I whispered, although there was no one there but us.

"When he went down for dinner, he told his cousin, who is a deputy, that if it came back capital, he was going to run. We need the deputies to bring him up in handcuffs and manacles." Margaret did not spook easily and was always very conscientious of her client's rights. This was out of character for her.

"Margaret, we can't do that. If the jury sees him in restraints, it will prejudice their thinking."

"I am sure about this. He may run."

"Then let him run," I retorted. "We'll get low, tell the deputies to aim high."

"Come on," she said and grabbed me by the arm.

The judge was sitting at his desk eating take-out when we knocked at his open door. Margaret explained what had occurred between our client and his cousin.

I interrupted. "Judge, we cannot bring him up in handcuffs and manacles. It will prejudice the jury if they come in seeing him like that."

The judge gave a knowing smile and nodded. "We'll bring him up in manacles only, and have him seated before the jury comes in. They will not see the restraints." I consented to the solution.

About an hour after the jury had returned from their dinner break and reconvened their discussions, they announced that they had a verdict. The bailiff handed a white piece of paper that he had received from the jury foreman to the judge.

"We, the jury," read the judge, "find the defendant guilty of Murder." The judge frowned. It was not capital murder, just plain murder. Bad enough, but the second trial for sentencing would not be necessary. Death was off the table. The judge polled the jurors asking each if it was their individual decision. All concurred.

The deputies took our client back to jail, and the jurors, judge, and district attorney quickly left the courtroom. I was sitting, gathering paperwork and files, war-weary, when a newspaper reporter entered the courtroom asking us for a comment on the ruling. She had been squirreled away in the press box at the back of the courtroom.

"We are happy with the verdict, given the circumstances," Margaret began. "Now, off the record?"

The reporter nodded. She had followed several of Margaret's trials, and they had an agreement — Margaret would give her insight if she would not publish certain things.

"Our client told his cousin that if the jury came back with capital murder, he was going to run, and take one of us with him as a hostage."

"What!" I shouted, "You did not tell me that part! Who was sitting next to the hall door from him; who could he tuck up under his arm like a football? You did not tell me that part …"

Umbraphilia and the Loss of Innocence
Katie Lamar Jackson

I remember my first time.

It lasted only two minutes and forty seconds and occurred in broad daylight beside an airport runway. I was fifty-nine years old and certainly no ingénue, but this experience was new and it fundamentally altered me, made me more worldly, and left me wanting more.

I am not speaking of a romantic or indecorous encounter, at least not in the corporal sense, but of the sublime experience of standing in the shadow of a total solar eclipse. This particular eclipse occurred on August 21, 2017, when the moon crossed in front of the sun, blocking its light and slowly unfurling a swath of shadow (known in technical eclipse jargon as a "path of totality" or "umbra") in a fifty-mile-wide ribbon across fourteen states. It was not a rare event — total eclipses happen somewhere in the world every eighteen months or so — but it was the first time since 1979 that a total eclipse could be seen in the U.S. and its shadowy path would come right across Tennessee, Georgia, and South Carolina, all states within an easy drive of my home in Opelika.

I could have seen the edges of the eclipse, the lighter gray area known as the penumbra that can reach out some thousand miles beyond the path of totality, from Opelika. In fact, I would have been perfectly satisfied to do so except for my husband, Kevin, who was determined to stand in this particular umbra.

A latent amateur astronomer (had he not become a doctor I think he might well have pursued a career in astrophysics), Kevin has always insisted we pause in our daily life to appreciate cosmic events such as meteor showers, super blood moons, comets, alignments of planets, and the like. He was in the throes of medical school when a total eclipse threw its shadow across Alabama in 1979 so he missed seeing it entirely. He also missed seeing an annular eclipse and its "ring of fire" in 1983 because he was working. But Kevin was determined to see this one.

"We'll probably never get to see one again," he said.

Resolved not to miss this "once-in-a-lifetime" opportunity, we rented a house in Fannin County, Georgia, and convinced several friends to join us. We were all eclipse "virgins," a term for first-time viewers, and all of us were looking forward to losing our eclipse innocence. Kevin, however, was passionate about ensuring our first time would be perfect, so he and I arrived three days before the eclipse to scout out the ideal viewing location.

The two of us rode up and down backroads, me at the wheel of the car while Kevin used GPS and eclipse-chasing technology to find a prime site in the path of totality, which led us to Martin Campbell Airfield, a small private airstrip located on the top of a plateau overlooking Ducktown and Copperhill, Tennessee.

When we pulled into the airport's parking lot, we were greeted by one of its owners, a Tom Selleck-handsome Vietnam veteran who told us he was hosting a number of locals there on eclipse day but who graciously said our small group of total strangers was more than welcome to join the gathering.

The Mystic Memoir

The day of the eclipse, our entourage arrived early to claim a spot on the grounds and set up our viewing equipment, lawn chairs, picnic baskets, and coolers. Soon more people arrived and by noon some seventy-five or so of us were poised to experience the eclipse.

Kevin turned on his "Solar Eclipse Timer," a phone app developed by an Alabamian named Gordon Telepun, a plastic surgeon with a passion for eclipse-gazing. The app was designed to prompt listeners to look for each phase of the eclipse including phenomena: diamond-like specks called Baily's Beads that pop out on the sides of the moon as it fully covers the sun, shadow bands that wriggle across the ground like spectral snakes, changes in air temperatures and wind, super-saturated colors in the landscape, and the reaction of animals as the sky darkens. (Day-dwelling birds go to roost and wildlife and livestock settle in to sleep while bats and other nocturnal creatures awaken. Even the noisy summer cicadas go quiet as the night-calling crickets and katydids start to sing.)

Throughout the morning, our airfield gathering had been a noisy place as people peered at the sun through protective eclipse glasses and chattered, laughed, and played music; "Total Eclipse of the Sun" and "You're so Vain" were quite popular. But as the moment of full totality approached, we humans grew quiet, our voices dropping to whispers. When the app announced, "Five. Four. Three, Two. One. Glasses off! Glasses off!" everyone fell silent and most remained that way for the entire one hundred and sixty seconds of full umbra.

In those seconds, I think we all fully grasped the deeply spiritual miracle of an eclipse.

I'd always heard about the moon's power over humans; how it can make us do crazy things. I now know that lunacy is real. That 2017 eclipse transformed many of us from normal, everyday humans into "umbraphiles," people so smitten by an eclipse experience that they will literally go to the ends of the earth to stand in its shadow.

Though Kevin and I have not chased every eclipse since, we did go to Chile and Argentina in July of 2019 to share an eclipse with several hundred people and a herd of llamas. And in 2023, we traveled to New Mexico where, along with a garrulous local cowboy and his red roan horse, Old Smokey, we watched as an annular eclipse created its ring of fire in the sky above.

There may be more eclipse experiences in our future. I hope so. But one thing is certain: once is not enough.

Road Trip with the Mystics
Margee Bright Ragland

One of my favorite trips was our tour of Northern Mississippi, hosted by our friend Rheta Grimsley Johnson. After a joyous gathering and readings from our latest book, *The Ploy of Cooking*, our Queen Gail and Mystic Joanne were designated to stay at Rheta's guest house that could accommodate two guests. Mystic Judith (now a Mystic Emeritus) and I were sent off to Rheta's friend, Ann, to spend the night in her guest cottage.

The cottage was a modest dwelling behind Ann's house. Entering the cottage, we observed a queen size bed dominating the room. An opening on the left side of the bed led to the bathroom. The opening on the right side led to the kitchen containing a small refrigerator and stove. Guarding the entrance to the kitchen was a life-size cutout of a Power Ranger, the one dressed in red. This guy never failed to frighten us every time we entered the cottage.

Earlier that afternoon, Judith and I had deposited our luggage at the cottage. Being gracious guests, we presented Ann with a large wheel of brie cheese and a bottle of pinot noir. Ann thanked us, putting the wheel of brie in the refrigerator in her house. She also introduced us to her Irish Wolfhound, Laddie, warning us that he was very protective of her, but he usually did not bite women, so no worries. Laddie gave us a bark and a low growl. Welcome to Ann's place.

On our return that evening, Ann bid us good night and retired to her house. She told us the fridge in the cottage was stocked and to help ourselves. As Judith and I relaxed after a day full of excitement, we decided to have a snack from the kitchen. Opening the fridge, we found it was stocked but only with bottles of vodka. We had held back a bottle of wine just in case, but we had no food. Why did we give Ann the brie? Could we retrieve it from her kitchen?

Making our way to the back door of her house and peering through the glass on the back door we were greeted by, guess who? Right, Laddie.

"Hi Laddie, good dog."

"Grrrrrrrrrr," replied Laddie, ears back and teeth showing.

Did I mention Laddie was quite large as well as being ferocious?

We decided to go around to the front of Ann's house and knock on her bedroom window.

It was now about 1:00 a.m. and no one was stirring in Iuka, Mississippi, except for Judith and me.

Peering out of Ann's bedroom window was another life size figure. This one was Hillary Clinton.

We peeked around Hillary to observe Ann in a sound sleep. We knocked and then threw little rocks at the window, but there was no way to rouse Ann.

We decided to return to the back door. Maybe Laddie had gone to sleep! Unfortunately, Laddie was ever vigilant. So we returned to the cottage. Frightened again by the Power Ranger, we drank our wine and resolved to go to sleep and dream of breakfast in the morning.

Chapter 7
Wearing Our Trousers Rolled

The Postman at Sunset
Gail Smith Langley

The postman comes late.
The elder people struggle
Through the chilling of day
Haltingly stepping at length
Gathering parceled and penned.

I am not provoked by a tardy arrival.
A small walk through old-stand trees
With glimpses of neighbor fellows
Collecting, perhaps, a rare letter
Among the unsolicited rubble.

Tonight, through the ancient growth,
Both pine and hardwood, erupts the sun's encore,
Cumulus strokes of vermillion, coral,
Carmine, garnet, russet, magenta.
Recompense, atonement, and redemption.

Walking with Nostalgia
Mary Dansak

I am often overwhelmed by nostalgia, especially at Christmas time. The ghosts of my mother and my little self drag me out of the present with each step of the holiday decorating. We are again tiptoeing into the Lutheran church with candles in our hands to sing carols at midnight, gathering magnolia and holly boughs to decorate the mantle, polishing silver bowls and tying red ribbons on candlesticks, my mother and me together, just us. My brother and father were not interested.

As I grew older, this intense nostalgic crush started happening in the summertime as well, particularly when I cut fruit. I could barely slice an apple without falling into reverie. As soon as the blade touched the peel, I was transported to summers of my early childhood, running errands with my mother, looking for the crispest apples and sweetest plums. Perplexed, I finally called my mother to tell her what my brain was doing.

"You're having a Proustian experience," she said. She was such a fan of Marcel Proust that she named her metal-framed walker Marcel. I listened as I bit into a perfect pear.

My mother died four months after this conversation. Decorating the Christmas tree that year was soul-wrenching and cathartic. There we were, back at the flower store buying green wire and Styrofoam cones. There we were, sprinkling red sugar crystals on warm cookies. Honoring our ritual of hanging two thousand strands of icicle tinsel on the tree one by one gave me two thousand discrete moments to be alone again with my mother.

Once the tree shimmered and sparkled to my liking, I purchased and wrapped Proust's six-volume novel *Remembrance of Things Past* (*In Search of Lost Time*) and put it under the tree for myself. I read the first two volumes, each weighty tomes of rich and evocative memories of some life I never lived. I imagined my mother reading the same words, as if she and I read them together. How very strange, how touched by the divine.

Hounded by its persistence, I looked up the word "nostalgia." It comes from the Greek root "*nostos*" meaning "return to home," and "*algos*" meaning "pain." The word was coined by a Swedish doctor in 1688 to describe the homesick condition of Swiss mercenary soldiers. To combat this malady, doctors concocted a treatment of leeches, opium, and a return to the Alps. These soldiers, I thought, they were missing their mamas.

As with most things worth pondering, nostalgia is complicated. Brain imaging shows that four distinct areas light up when we experience its pull. Paradoxically, the brain perceives nostalgia as both novel and familiar, giving it a double-edged superpower on our emotions. There must be some evolutionary advantage for this mystical longing, but what?

Maybe it's like glue, keeping our present selves psychically connected to our past selves in a way that memory alone cannot. After all, a body is merely a collection of atoms squashed together at a given moment in time, with atoms constantly flowing in and out. Despite DNA's persistent instruction, we are in a constant state of flux.

Sometimes my memories have nothing to do with the phantom nostalgia I experience. Did I shop on Fifth Avenue, twirling in the snow, elbows bent with the weight of my Saks and FAO Schwartz bags? Did I ride on a sleigh behind a team of Clydesdales, bells chiming in my ears, through a wintry landscape? Did I play a rousing game of football with my cousins after a holiday feast? No. Yet nostalgia leaves me atingle with a fuzzy longing for these events from an imaginary past.

Time passes, bringing more Decembers, the calendar being reliable and sound. I honor the Christmas traditions I have set for myself. Every year, after hanging all the ornaments on the tree, I settle in for the careful placement of two thousand strands of tinsel. I look forward to walking hand-in-hand with my mother during this days-long ritual. I welcome an indescribable state of mind.

Muffuletta
Joanne Camp

"Hey, Jo-Nan." Johndrow nudged me. Despite being lawyers, we were both sitting behind the bar, that railing that separates the attorneys and legal personnel from the onlookers, awaiting the court to call our cases.

"The judge just called you." She indicated with her elbow toward the bench. Both her hands were on her cell phone as she continued to text.

I looked up from the report I had been reading. The judge, his court reporter, and the juvenile court clerk were all looking at me. I stood, and responded in a respectful "Sir?" The judge sat on a raised platform three feet above the courtroom floor, surrounded by wooden beadboard that corralled his desk.

As the judge continued, "How long do you think your case will take, Ms. Camp? We may need to reschedule." I concentrated on his lips; they were moving, but I could not make out exactly what he was saying. The clerk intervened.

"Judge, that case should be short. It's the Montgomery case that will take almost all day."

"All right, then, continue that case until Friday, and we'll adjourn until after lunch with your case, Ms. Camp."

As we filed out of the courtroom, the bailiff at the door winked at me. "Fall asleep?" he smiled.

"Pardon?"

He repeated himself.

"No," I laughed, "just deep into that DHR report."

From my mother, my sisters and I inherited a toothy smile, a thick head of hair, and hearing loss. I would visit my mother, in her later years, in the duplex she purchased after my father died, moving out of the big house when her twelve children finally all flew the nest. If the television was on, it boomed throughout the small living and kitchen area. The volume had to be lowered before any conversation could begin. Even in a face-to-face conversation, I noticed a concentration on her face as she tried to interpret what I was saying.

I would gently prod, "Mom, why don't you get your hearing checked?"

When she would complain about the new pastor mumbling, I again would prompt, "Mom, the advancements they have made in hearing aids are remarkable."

After years of such urging, she finally asked, "Joanne, what makes you think I want to hear?"

The next to fall was my younger sister, Kathy. Although she had little post-secondary education, she had worked her way through the ranks from secretary to officer of the bank. While in charge of a branch when the higher-ups were off at a conference, a young teller, wringing her hands, approached Kathy's desk.

"Ms. Kathy, what should we do?"

"What should we do about what?" she replied.

"The alarm, Ms. Kathy, the alarm is going off."

It appeared that the hearing deficit was tone based. While I could hear most people, if there was no background noise, I could not make out what Judge was saying without concentration and lipreading. One day, frustrated, during a conference with other attorneys and the judge, I exclaimed,

"Judge, you and I should be married ..." He gave me a puzzled look. "Because I have become completely tone-deaf to the sound of your voice."

When the decline began, I could not determine. When my children were younger, I had the hearing of a greater wax moth. To whispers about forbidden activities in a room down a hallway, I would respond, "Don't even think it!" When my younger son slipped into the pantry and stealthily tried to open a cookie package, I ordered, "not before dinner." To which he replied, "How do you KNOW?" And once when my teen tried to sneak out, I heard the swoosh of the downstairs window opening from the upstairs bedroom and was able to intercept him at the corner of the house.

But now genetics and age had taken that ability away and replaced it with tinnitus — the sound of tree frogs and cicadas. In the audiologist's sound booth, with an apparatus in my hand and the instructions of the audiologist in my mind to "press the button when you hear a tone," for a long while all I heard was my symphony of night critters. Then, finally, through the muffle, a tiny sound pierced the quiet. Then another. But soon they dissolved into my background noise. Then a deeper timbre crescendoed and faded again.

After a series of sounds hummed in each ear, the audiologist's voice crackled in my headphones with the request to repeat each word after her: "Read, Pan, Food, Tire, Ring, Ditch, Red, Luck ..." Some of the words I understood; some left me guessing. When the testing was done, she smiled, took me to a conference room, explained the test results, and introduced me to the remarkable advancements of hearing aids, advancements that came with their own sticker shock.

When the instruments arrived, I wore them religiously but did not let anyone, not even my other hard-of-hearing sisters, know of my new gadgets. The aids tucked neatly behind my ears hidden by that inherited full head of hair. A nearly invisible tube connected the earpiece with the device. No visible change, but the world had become so loud. The rustle of leaves in the trees, the whine of tires on the road, the hiss of the air-conditioning vents. But there was also the whisper of a sister's secret, a called greeting of a friend, and the clarity of an instructor's lesson. Gradually, though, family and co-workers noticed my new-found attention.

While the ability to hear clearly again is wonderful, at the end of a long day, as I crawl into bed and remove my hearing aids, the world softens, sounds muffle again, and I relax into a cocoon of quiet. Because sometimes, "what makes you think I want to hear?"

Studio 521
Margee Bright Ragland

In March of 2021, a mid-century modern house two blocks from my home had a "For Sale" sign in the yard. I had been admiring this house for years, so I immediately called the phone number on the sign. The seller was the owner. Unfortunately, she told me that an offer had already been made on the house. I gave her my number and urged her to call me if the sale fell through.

I thought, oh well, do I really want another studio? I should mention that I already own a `60s ranch house on the same street that was briefly my studio. However, five years ago, one of my children moved back to Auburn. So, guess who lives in my former studio? Okay, he has a place to live, and I'm happy he's back in Auburn.

To my surprise, the owner called me the next day and asked me if I wanted to see the house. Of course, I wanted to see the house, and I loved the interior as much as the exterior. Lori, the owner, could see it was love at first sight for me. She said, "I want you to have this house."

I talked to my husband about my desire to purchase another house, and he said, "You're seventy-three years old. How long are you going to wait to have your own studio?" So, within a week with a bit of negotiating, I purchased the perfect studio, number 521 Cherokee Lane.

I methodically organized all my art supplies that occupied our front bedroom. Little by little I moved everything to my new space. That bedroom is now restored to its original purpose ... a guest bedroom. Finally, we can have overnight guests and no one can accuse me of being a hoarder.

Studio 521 has become "Margee's Playhouse." I decorated with the help of Wayfare, Hayneedle, and Etsy. Also, the studio holds my fun work-in-progress, a life-sized assemblage. The studio at 521 is a perfect place to work on large commissioned portraits.

My one problem was the yard. My husband and I own one battery-powered lawn mower. This is moved between four houses by an ancient and unreliable Toyota Tacoma pickup truck. I decided to order another mower just for the studio.

As I waited for the mower delivery from Lowes, the grass was growing. Suddenly a young man knocked on the door. "Can I mow your yard?" he said. "My name is David, and I am starting my own business."

I stared at a trailer parked out front that was carrying a large riding lawn mower ready for action. "How much?" I asked.

"For the front yard, $20. Same for the back."

"Go for it, David." I responded.

David cut my front yard in a matter of minutes and headed to the back yard. Unfortunately, his lawn mower was too large to fit through the backyard gate. He knocked on my door to make me aware of his dilemma.

"Okay, instead of mowing my back yard head up the street to 539. That's my other house on the street."

That 539 house is only three lots away from 521. Still, I didn't hear David on his mower or see his rig. I figured I better run up the street and see where my yard guy was. As I ran by 539, I heard a mower in the distance. David was at 569 happily mowing away. Waving my arms I shouted, "Stop David! Wrong house!" He finally noticed me, after mowing half of a lawn that was still totally overgrown. He stopped, loaded up, and headed back down to 539.

I had no idea who lived at 569 where there was now a half-mowed lawn. I wasn't about to find out. Hopefully they were not trying to have a "natural" yard with wildflowers and abundant plants.

David successfully mowed my second yard. I paid him $10 more for his misguided efforts. He loaded up and headed out in search of more lawns to support his new business.

The next day my new lawn mower arrived from Lowes. I have now mowed my front and back yards as well as battled the English ivy and wisteria that threatened to take over my house and the yard.

I am determined to try to take care of my new studio all by myself. My thanks go out to David for the memory of the mistaken lawn. I wish him great success with his new business.

Missed Notes
Gail Smith Langley

I must have been eight or nine years old when I was introduced to piano lessons by my sober instructor, Mrs. Andrews. I assume that I tortured Mrs. Andrews for several months, as she sat rigid against a battery of missed notes. Not far into my musical education, my lessons were abruptly terminated by my instructor who alerted my mother to my musical inadequacies.

In her quiet yet somehow stern voice, Mrs. Andrews delivered the cruel hammer with this message: "Most of my students have a modicum of talent for the piano. This is not the case here. Perhaps you might like to save your money?"

Consequently, at an early age my visions of Carnegie Hall were incontestably stifled. I had not even conquered "Chop Sticks" from John Thompson's First Grade Book, much less "Spinning Song," a recital favorite of the more talented. I was abruptly whisked away into the fate of the tone-deaf. (Footnote: I actually had never heard of Carnegie Hall at the time, but if I had, I now realized that I would never take that stage ... not as a pianist anyway.) Had fame eluded me? Maybe I could be a movie star and hang out with Sal Mineo and Tab Hunter?

Through the years, my brush with music continued on a sharply declining path. Miss Bright, my elementary school music teacher, demoted me to playing the lone triangle in fipple-flute recorder class. The other children continued on, flouting away to "Row, Row, Row Your Boat" while I could tap the triangle at the first, and only the first, "merrily." Musically, I was way downstream from the rest of the class.

In college, I took up guitar in order to play The Kingston Trio and Joan Baez songs. My hip college friends would suddenly recall a next-day exam to make a stealthy exit during my earnest performance of "The Answer, My Friend, Is Blowing in the Wind."

I was tapping on the door of my symphonic-deficient seventh decade when the thought struck me ... Mrs. Andrews was right, music ability was left out of my double helix. But, on my twisted genetic ladder is an overabundance of stick-to-it-iveness, tenacity, orneriness, and a double gene helping of obstinacy. Thinking about it, I am probably a prodigy in mule-headed stubbornness. Surely these sterling qualities can substitute for God-given talent in keyboard skills?

Perhaps I could learn a musical instrument by will power, so I encouraged the long- suffering husband to buy a keyboard for my Christmas gift. My selection was a Yamaha that could most likely launch the space station. The machine came with a thirty-page instruction book as well as an abundance of function buttons. Push one and an entire orchestra will accompany "Are you sleeping, Brother John? Ding. Dong. Ding." All of these at-hand accessories I largely ignored while shades of Mrs. Andrews' annoyance danced in my head.

I dove right into learning the elementary songs that I had mostly ignored in my first piano book, "Happy Birthday," "Ode to Joy," "Twinkle, Twinkle, Little Star," and "Für Elise." Encouraged by these simple arrangements, I moved on to the more difficult "Do Lord, oh, do Lord, oh, do remember me." I found this to be above my new-found skill. "Certainly, if I played the notes over and over, I would learn this song," I surmised. At one point, I paused in my stick-to-it-iveness of pounding wrong notes to notice, through the window, the husband was sitting in his truck possibly enjoying a brew. It was early morning. Did I detect cotton in his ears?

I have shared my sad untalented story with friends. As it turns out, many of them had similar experiences. The most striking of these recounts came from a fellow writer. As she sat playing scales and struggling though "On Top of Old Smokey," the teacher was in the next room cooking supper. In order to earn her pay, the apron-clad tutor would occasionally lean through the door with her wooden spoon as a baton and count, "And a one and a two."

I had a visit from my friend, Ann, an accomplished pianist. I recounted my piano instructor story, a dismal tale of woe, and exclaimed how I had overcome my reluctance to become skillful on the black and whites. Also, I confided that I thought the husband was going to divorce me over "Do Lord."

"Why don't you buy some earphones?" my friend inquired.

"Earphones?" I exclaimed. "Earphones?" I continued, "There were no earphones in the box."

"Perhaps Yamaha was not planning on 'Do Lordy,'" Ann replied. "You can buy a set and plug them right into the back of the keyboard."

In an emergency effort to save a declining marriage, I ordered the earphones immediately, splurging on one-day delivery. Consequently, I am happily banging away, and for all anyone knows, I am playing symphonies. Seriously, although "Do Lord remember me" has not been attained, the marriage will go on and on along with my heart.

Beyond-the-Grave Greens
Mary Dansak

Collard greens remind me of my father. He used to make them up in the big silver pressure cooker with a hissing and jiggling valve on the lid. As the house filled with the stench of cooking greens, he'd wrinkle his nose and say, "Smell that pot likker?" I didn't like greens when I was little. I'd eat around them at dinner time, and my awful brother would sneak his stinky greens onto my plate when the grown-ups weren't paying attention, which was all the time.

Along about the time I turned thirty my taste buds changed, and I began to love Daddy's greens. Every New Year's Day I could expect the call from him. "Did you eat your black-eyed peas and collards?" That was the invitation to come out to the house for our good luck sustenance. We'd pile into the kitchen, me, my husband, our three little girls and some dogs, to be greeted by the rascally stench of pot likker and Janie's about-to-burn cornbread in the oven. "Smells good, Daddy," I'd say. His collards were the best-ever. I kept meaning to pay attention to how he made them.

"Jose," he'd say to my husband Joe, "can I get you a snort?" Then he'd pour himself a drink: one jigger of Evil Willie, one jigger of water, three ice cubes.

Daddy died in 2016 after a decline which began on New Year's Eve. He was in the ICU on New Year's Day, and I'm quite sure he didn't get his Hoppin John, bad luck which would portend his death nine months later. Now, New Year's Days are poignant reminders that he is gone. While he did give me the exact and perfect recipe for his nightly toddy, he did not impart to me the recipe for the greens. All I know is that he cooked them in the pressure cooker, and he threw in a pinch of sugar, like he did to all his vegetables.

Forgive me, but after Daddy died, I resorted to canned Glory brand greens for our New Year's Day breakfasts. They're not bad. I confessed to a friend that I liked them almost as much as Daddy's greens and was scolded sharply. "Don't you EVER tell anyone you like store-bought greens as much as your daddy's!" Ouch.

Among other life changes, that global pandemic had Joe and me, now empty-nesters, cooking at home. Joe got interested in comfort food: meat loaf, mashed potatoes, and collard greens. I was eager to make the meat and potatoes, but no way was I making the greens. I'd never live up to my dad's recipe. Joe's were okay, but nothing like the standard I'd set.

And then I had the dream. I was up to my elbows in the kitchen when Daddy walked into the room. In this dream there was no feeling of impending doom or strangeness that often accompanies dreams about the dead. He simply showed up and did some cooking, patiently teaching me how to make the perfect collards. Finally, I'd have his recipe! But dang if I still didn't pay attention! I awoke as clueless as ever.

The next time Joe came home with the makings for our favorite pandemic feast, I got busy with my part while Joe retired to the bedroom.

"Come make the greens," I called.

"Let's make them in that fancy new thing you got," he called back, meaning the Instant Pot. I don't have a big silver pressure cooker with a jiggly valve on the lid. Despite the word "let's,"

Joe did not come forth from the bedroom, where he had his nose to his phone reading the latest on the dastardly virus.

Emboldened by the dream-visit from my father, I decided I could do it. Maybe I didn't have the recipe, but I had the spirit.

I massaged the greens with olive oil and apple cider vinegar, something I'm sure my Daddy never did. "Don't judge. I don't know your magic tricks," I said out loud to any ghostly presence who might have been looking over my shoulder. For all I know, he too was led by the spirit. He probably didn't even have a recipe. I threw in some salt, a dash of this and that, and eschewed the ham all together. "There are such things as vegetarian vegetables," I insisted.

I squished the massaged and seasoned collards down into the Instant Pot and locked the lid. "Good luck in there," I whispered insanely.

It turned out my greens were delicious. All I needed was a little push from beyond the grave to make them mine.

A Leaper of Waves Grown Old
Gail Smith Langley

Here the gulf can be traumatized by the storms
And worried by the closeness of the Mobile Bay.
It is not often that the waters are glass
from shore to bottom.
But today, the gulf is beguilingly clear and autumnly chilled.

There are a few sets of families taken to the ocean,
But I stay in shore where I have anchored my chair.
The young children are in shrilled voice vaulting the waves.
They have sidelined me from my book without objection.

I was a swimmer of oceans and a fighter of waves.
Yet now, I am content to watch the young ones in their glee.
If I find it again in such rare form, the beautiful gulf,
And if the weather warms, perhaps I will go again to the sea.

Music of the Spheres
Marian Carcache

How in the world can I write about old age when in my heart I am not there yet?

The looking glass belies my delusions, so I've stopped allowing it to reflect me. The Amish have the right idea about mirrors. And we should all take a lesson from Narcissus and *The Snow Queen*. Mirrors can paralyze us, or worse, freeze our heart to ice.

Instead of applying my "Back to the Fuchsia" lipstick and "Electroshock Blue" eye shadow this morning, I am sitting on Highlands, the cement back porch of my studio, wearing a summer nightgown I inherited when a loved one died, indulging in a second cup of coffee. It's Mama Mocha's Vienna roast, and, like me, it has a buttery body and a muted acidity. Unlike me, it also has a clearly defined sheen. Ironically, or maybe significantly, my favorite bean is called Old Timer.

The dogs are digging up the back yard while I listen to The Avett Brothers singing "No Hard Feelings." It would be a perfect goodbye song to leave the world on. But I am not ready to leave the earth just yet. I add the song to my funeral playlist.

A volunteer squash has come up in the middle of yard, proudly displaying its billowing yellow blooms. The climbing passionflowers have covered the fence and are looking for all the world like violet swimming pool ballerinas from an Esther Williams movie.

The chinaberry trees are covered in star-shaped purple flowers, the mimosas in pink powder puffs that compete with gardenias and tea olive for the most heavenly scent on earth.

Later tonight, when I will take the dogs out before bedtime, we'll walk barefooted through the four o'clocks that fill the summer evening breeze with their sweet scent. While the dogs sniff around for the *very* best places, I will talk to the stars that I have come to believe represent my loved ones, dog and human, who have gone from my sight on earth.

I will thank them for making my life so much richer and hang onto the hope that I will be with them again someday, all of us rolled into one immortal dog bed of endless love.

Beautiful words, sweet scents and sounds, the taste of good coffee, my own backyard, the night sky, and most of all, those creatures I've loved so much along the way — the not-so-foul "rag and bone shop of my heart" — have left their mark and made the journey worth its price.

The Age of Potential
Katie Lamar Jackson

"Potential has a shelf life."

That's what a friend once said to me, in reference to a former boyfriend whose possibilities I had a hard time renouncing even after he made it very clear he saw no future in me.

But does potential really expire or is it just finally too exhausted to keep begging for attention? Or is it stolen from us by age and obsolescence?

These questions hound me and, I suspect, many of us who fall in the "of a certain age" category, a designation that usually includes women over the age of fifty; sixty maybe seventy or older if you're male. The answers shouldn't be that hard to find. After all, aging and the angst of aging is nothing new; I'd be willing to bet that my parents and grandparents and each generation before them worried about the limits aging placed upon them. Sure, sometimes those physical and mental confines are inflicted by the ravages of time, but all too often they are the havoc of a society that deems aging, especially in women, as an ending rather than as a beginning.

For me, the worries of aging first came truly knocking when I retired from my long-time university job at the relatively tender age of fifty-three. I was young for a retiree, but I felt old and useless. I also still needed and wanted to work, so I set about doing what I'd always wanted to do — working as a full-time freelance writer. Soon I had plenty of work, and as the jobs have continued to come in, none of my clients has ever asked to see my college transcripts or my Medicare card. It's been a successful second act so far.

During those early post-retirement months, I felt a renewed sense of excitement about my work, but with it I also began to feel something unfamiliar and a bit scary: a sense of mortality. Every ache and pain became a concern that niggled at my semi-consciousness with the tenacity of a Jack Russell terrier trying to worry a chipmunk out of its hole. What if my shelf life was expiring? Or what if whatever potential I had left, potential I had squandered for most of my life because I was doing other things, was about to be stolen away by some unexpected illness or tamped down by life's responsibilities?

These days I realize I wasted a lot of time worrying about mortality. After all, I've survived more than a decade now beyond that first retirement, and I am busy, too busy much of the time because I'm reluctant to say "no" to new projects that might build my retirement savings and resume. But honestly, at my age does a resume really need to be built? Something to think about ...

These days I'm also trying hard to say "no" more often and to live in the moment — to see the potential in every day — which oddly sometimes gives me time to reflect on who I used to be. Like when I was a kid of five or six years old and felt like I might explode with a sense of possibility. I remember it as a physical tightness that pressed out from my heart against my breastbone, rib cage, and throat with a tender, feral power.

It was excruciating. It was exquisite.

I'm pretty sure it was "potential" pleading to be set free, promising a future I believed existed but could not quite imagine. Or maybe it was might, as in strength but also as in "might be possible."

As I grew older, I think that feeling remained in me, but day-to-day living robbed it of its heat. Still, there have been times in my life when some external catalyst such as a new infatuation, the birth of a child, an exciting job offer, the sound of John Hiatt's voice ringing from my car radio, roused it awake. Sadly, it never woke up at a convenient time, and I'd shush it back to sleep, promising to come back one day soon and reawaken it. Let it out. But I never did.

Lately, though, I've felt it stirring. Maybe that's because I've been listening to Hiatt again and other voices from my past, those of Jerry Jeff Walker, John Prine, Patsy Cline, Nanci Griffith that remind me of my former selves, the "me" who used to laugh and cry and dance and be inspired by these tunes and sometimes even inspired by my own self.

Truth is, I don't want to go back to those former selves. I just don't want to forget them. Instead, I want to seize THIS age of potential. After all, I'm probably the best I will ever be.

Preparing to Migrate
Gail Smith Langley

It is September.
The miniature birds surround the sweetwater feeder
Landing and fleeting. Soaring and circling
Like an ever-changing Calder mobile
Just a momentary piece of beauty.
And I in my seventy-fifth year
Will be the keeper of this memory.
Soon the hummers will leave
Following an ancestor's path
Coursing to a finer winter place.
And, in a not-too-distant September,
I too will migrate.

MYSTIC BIOS

(Left to Right) Seated: Joanne Camp, Katie Lamar Jackson, Mary Dansak and Marian Carcache. Standing: Gail Langley, Margee Bright Ragland.

Gail Smith Langley: The Mystic Queen

    I grew up in Auburn, Alabama, in the shadow of API (Alabama Polytechnic Institute, now Auburn University) where my grandfather was the college's first librarian, and my father was an API football player. I still live near the college with husband Saint Bob. Our only child, Rivers Langley, has run off to Hollywood.
    I was a schoolteacher for many years until I became seriously allergic to children. I have also been an art and antique dealer.
    Along with my Mystic Order sisters, we have written several short story books including some questionable cookbooks. Without my sisters, I am the lone author of a children's book, *No Snake in the House Rule*.
    In my golden years, I read books through page fifty and continue if it suits me. I also travel with other women, who do not sit outside stores tapping their feet. I try my luck at bird identification, and then it is time to order dinner from a large selection of establishments who are kind enough to door delivery. Evening news. Jeopardy. Doze.

Joanne Camp: The Mystic Defender

    I am a recovering attorney who, after practicing law in Alabama for more than thirty-five years, am trying to retire to devote more time to my first love — writing — but occasionally relapse into law. My excuse is that the legal system is too rich a scavenging ground for my short stories. Before the Mystics, most of my fiction writing was limited to appellate briefs to the

Alabama Courts of Appeals and the eight novels I have in various stages of completion.

I have been married to my second love, Jimmy Camp, for forty-seven years. While trying to avoid my first love and its large white blank pages, we travel the countryside in a recreational vehicle we lovingly call "The Dry Boat." We have three adventurous grown sons: Jeremy, a virologist living in Austria; Michael, an environmental scientist scouring the woods around Tuscaloosa; and Jake, a computer tech trying to keep state departments in Montgomery up and running.

My husband and I live on a small farm in South Auburn where during the summer, we produce all the vegetables and fruit that we eat. Besides writing and the RV lifestyle, I enjoy hiking, foraging for edible mushrooms and weeds, traveling to Austria to visit my twin toddler grandchildren, and crocheting.

Marian Carcache: The Mystic Dog Whisperer

I grew up in rural Russell County, Alabama, between a pecan orchard and a rye grass field — with dogs for siblings. Retired from Auburn University, I teach American and global literature and several creative writing courses online for Southern New Hampshire University.

My fiction has been included in various literary journals and anthologies, and *Under the Arbor,* the opera based on one of my short stories, appeared on PBS stations nationwide. My collection of short stories, *The Moon and the Stars,* and my novella, *The Tongues of Men and Angels,* were published by Solomon and George Publishers. I also write a weekly column for a regional newspaper, *The Citizen of East Alabama,* and contribute to southern-themed magazines, including *Magnolia and Moonshine* and *Columbus and the Valley*.

I find joy spending time with my inspiring son, John David, a photographer and print maker, and my dogs, Grimm and Jazz.

Mary Dansak: The Nebulous Mystic

I'm a product of the Deep South, a tree-hugging, left-leaning, animal-loving writer and retired science education specialist. My husband, Joe, and our three dogs live in a house that looks like a tree stump where we've raised three radically brilliant daughters and are enjoying basking in the energy of our two critter-loving granddaughters.

As well as writing with the Mystic Order, I have a weekly column, "Little Green Notebook," which runs in our local paper. I'm a regular contributor to the magazine *Magnolia and Moonshine* and have done scriptwriting for the television show *Steve Trash Science*.

Semi-retired, I am happily employed as the chronicler of daily life on a horse and cattle ranch, where I spend luxurious hours atop a stunning buttercream Palomino named Jasper, spying on the ranch hands and animals. I am thrilled to be back in the saddle.

Katie Lamar Jackson: The Mystic Oracle

Possessed with a curious soul, I have always been intrigued by the stories of people and places, which is no doubt why I became a writer. It's a career that, for more than forty years now, has given me carte blanche to ask a lot questions, explore all manner of ideas and landscapes, and constantly take stock of the world around me.

Over those four-plus decades I've worked as a journalist, book author, communications specialist, and educator and have been able to write about everything from gardening to eclipse chasing, artists to scientists, and wilderness spaces to wild horses. In the process, I've published thousands of articles and, to date, eleven books on such diverse topics as a one-eyed fortuneteller, a Vietnam war hero, an Eighteenth-century explorer, and a woman-led environmental movement. It's been a blast so far and I hope to pen many more stories in the years to come.

When I'm not writing or thinking about writing, my husband Kevin and I spend as much time as possible appreciating the natural world outside our backdoor and in more far-flung places. I also spend lots of time chasing after my nine grandchildren, rewilding my yard, and taking photos of this big old amazing world we all share.

Margee Bright Ragland: The Mystic Illuminator

I'm a painter and teacher who, using a variety of different media, explores ideas and personal narratives that evolve as I make the work.

My educational background includes a BFA from Auburn University and an MVA from Georgia State University, where I served as Professor of Art for thirty years until my retirement in 2017. These days, I'm making art; dancing; traveling with my husband, Wayne; and spending time with our four children and three grandchildren.

As a member of the Mystic Order of East Alabama Fiction writers, I've illustrated and written for our four books and my own book, *Bright Illuminations: The Art of Margee Bright Ragland and the Words of Others*, a collection of forty-nine collages paired with the writing of twenty-seven authors.

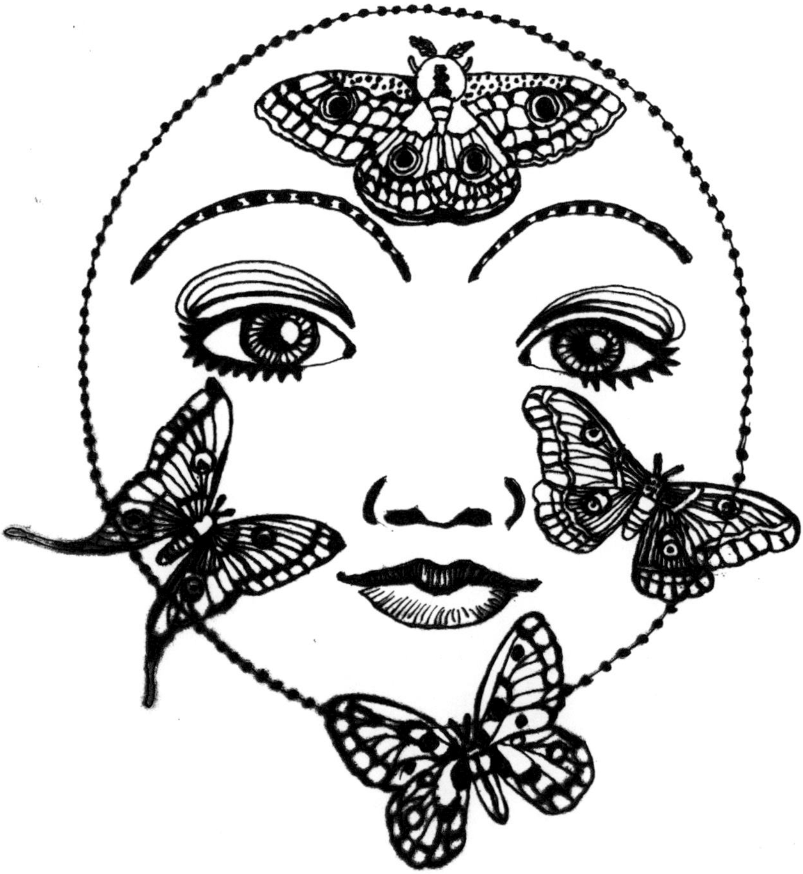

Made in the USA
Columbia, SC
24 December 2024